PRESCHOOLERS: QUESTIONS AND ANSWERS

PRESCHOOLERS: QUESTIONS AND ANSWERS

Psychoanalytic Consultations with Parents, Teachers, and Caregivers

ERNA FURMAN, EDITOR

INTERNATIONAL UNIVERSITIES PRESS, INC.
Madison   Connecticut

INTERNATIONAL UNIVERSITIES PRESS and IUP (& design) ® are registered trademarks of International Universities Prtess, Inc.

Library of Congress Cataloging-in-Publication Data

Preschoolers: questions and answers: psychoanalytic consultations
    with parents, teachers, and caregivers/Erna Furman, editor.
       p. cm.
    Includes bibliographical references and index.
    ISBN 0-8236-4255-0
    1. Child psychology, 2. Parent and child. 3. Preschool children-
-Counseling of. I. Furman, Erna.
BF721.P69 1995
155.42'3—dc20   95-8949
                                                             CIP

Manufactured in the United States of America

Contents

Contributors

CAROL EBER is a preschool teacher with degrees in elementary and early childhood education. Her teaching experience includes nine years of teaching in classrooms in the Cleveland area and Japan and, most recently, nineteen years as Head Teacher/Director of the Lyndhurst Cooperative Nursery School. In addition to her classroom work, she has attended ongoing seminars and courses at the Cleveland Center for Research in Child Development and has participated in a Consultation Group. She is currently conducting parent education sessions.

ERNA FURMAN is a nonmedical child psychoanalyst and licensed psychologist. She is a faculty member of the Cleveland Center for Research in Child Development's Course in Child Psychoanalysis, of the Cleveland Psychoanalytic Institute, and of the Department of Psychiatry, Case Western Reverve University School of Medicine. As a qualified teacher, she has taught at all levels and is especially active in applying psychoanalytic findings in the field of education. She treats children and works with parents at the Hanna Perkins School, is the Director of its Toddler Groups, and has conducted the Center's research projects.

ROBERT A. FURMAN, M.D., is Director Emeritus of the Cleveland Center for Research in Child Development and of the Hanna Perkins Therapeutic School, having been in charge of their many programs and activities for some thirty years. He is also a training analyst in child and adult psychoanalysis at the Cleveland Psychoanalytic Institute, a faculty member of Case Western Reserve University School of Medicine, and was a board-certified pediatrician. In addition to his ongoing work with patients and with the Center's Consultation Groups, he has served in a number of professional organizations and was President of the Association for Child Psychoanalysis.

RUTH HALL is Director of Therapy at the Hanna Perkins School and a faculty member of the Cleveland Center for Research in Child

Development's Course in Child Psychoanalysis. She is a nonmedical child psychoanalyst as well as an experienced speech therapist and specialist in speech pathlogy. In addition to her psychoanalytic work with children and parents, she has been very active as teacher and consultant in the Center's Extension Service.

YVETTE ANNE HOFFMAN has served as Staff Nurse for the Cleveland Visiting Nurse Association. Through her parental involvement with the Solon Cooperative Preschool, she became a preschool educator and earned a master's degree in early child education. She participated in a Consultation Group of the Cleveland Center for Research in Child Development for many years. In addition, she served in various positions on the Executive Board of the Cleveland Association for the Education of Young Children. Upon her retirement as Director/Teacher of the Solon Cooperative Preschool, she has continued her interest in young children as a Docent in the Education Departments of the Cleveland Metroparks Zoo and the Cleveland Orchestra.

LUANE RAIA LASKY holds a bachelor's degree in music education and a master's degree in curriculum and instruction. She worked for many years as Director/Teacher of the Lyndhurst Cooperative Preschool and participated in a Consultation Group of the Cleveland Center for Research in Child Development. At the present time, Mrs. Lasky is Director of a public school string music program at elementary and secondary levels.

KATE O'ROURKE holds a degree in early childhood education and psychology, with postgraduate work at the Merrill Palmer Institute in Detroit. She is presently the Director of the Special Horizon Early Intervention Center in North Olmstead where she is teaching preschool and the Mother and Toddler Discovery Program. Past experiences include similar commitments at the Glenview Center and Parkview Preschool. She has attended several courses of the Cleveland Center for Research in Child Development and participated in a Consultation Group.

NANCY SABATH is a preschool educator with degrees in early childhood curriculum and supervision. She has been Director of a preschool program, Head Kindergarten Teacher of the Hanna Perkins Therapeutic School, and College Instructor in Early Childhood Education. She has also been an Instructor in the Cleveland Center for Research in Child Development's Extension Service and is an

active member of its Advisory Committee. Currently, Mrs. Sabath is the Disabilities–Mental Health Coordinator of a county
wide Head Start Program.

EDWARD J. SCHIFF, M.D., is a training analyst in child and adult psychoanalysis at the Cleveland Psychoanalytic Institute and a member
of its Educational Committee. He is also on the faculty of the
Department of Psychiatry of Case Western Reserve University
School of Medicine. In addition to his clinical practice and teaching commitments, he has been a long-standing participant in the
work of the Hanna Perkins School, of the Cleveland Center for
Research in Child Development, of its Extension Service and
research projects.

BARBARA WELCH holds a B.A. in education, with additional courses
at Ursuline College. Having initially worked as an elementary
school teacher, she has, for many years now, devoted herself to
preschool education. She was the Director of her own Church of
The Master Nursery School as well as Teacher and Head Teacher
at other preschools and, for several years, participated in a Consultation Group of the Cleveland Center for Research in Child
Development.

Preface

This volume, like the earlier *What Nursery School Teachers Ask Us About* (1986c), derives its contents from two sources: our child analysts' intensive long-term work with individual children and their families at the Hanna Perkins Therapeutic School (R. A. Furman and A. Katan, 1969) and Child-Analytic Clinic of its twin agency, the Cleveland Center for Research in Child Development; and the sharing and application of the findings through our Extension Service in which we work with other professionals, such as preschool educators, caregivers, elementary and high-school teachers, pediatricians, child life workers, and others who serve and care for children.

Both kinds of work have been ongoing since the early 1950s, but during the last ten or so years, there have also been some changes. Our School and Center have benefited from the added experience with our Mother-Toddler Group (E. Furman, 1992, 1993). Many community educators have, likewise, included toddler groups in their nursery and daycare settings, and many more of them have participated in our courses, consultation groups, and on-site consultation service. Also, our Child Development-Parenting Course (E. Furman, 1987a,b) for adolescent parents and their children have enabled us to learn about and assist yet many more of the very young. As a result, we have not only continued to deepen our understanding of preschoolers, kindergarteners, and older children, but have gained new insights about the development of toddlers and the special tasks that face their parents and parent substitutes.

Since 1969, our Annual Workshop for Preschool Educators, Caregivers and Mental Health Professionals has provided a regular yearly opportunity for all the Center faculty and Extension Service participants to meet. Thanks to the repeated generosity of Mrs. Eugenie Radney of Akron, these workshops are free of charge. They are a format for presenting and discussing areas of current concern to all of us who work with children. Workshop topics are selected from the ongoing work of the various Extension Service activities during the preceding year. They reflect the problems and questions educators and child specialists bring for discussion, new understandings jointly gained, and new approaches tried in assisting children and parents. Since other publications on these topics are, for the most part not approached with dynamic understanding, we also put them in writing, as pamphlets distributed through our Center. Many participants wanted to reread and rethink them at leisure and share them with their colleagues as well as with the parents of their charges.

The chapters in this book are primarily a selection of these workshop topics—an attempt to share our thinking and feeling with parents and professionals, all those who, like ourselves, care for and about children and their families.

Ours is *the* impossible profession. Those who proclaim to know all the answers and have ready prescriptions, with statistics and jargon to couch them in, have looked at child development, at parenting, at education, from the outside. Those who have lived in and with the work appreciate only too well that children grow in their very own ways. We can at best facilitate their path. Rather than ''making them'' or making them fit into prearranged pigeonholes, we have to think and feel with each one and build a relationship of safety and trust that will allow them to consider and perhaps use what we have to offer.

In the same spirit, this book offers our experiences and efforts at understanding—not to indoctrinate or even to persuade, but as ways of learning and making sense of the myriad puzzlements, concerns, satisfactions, and frustrations we encounter day in, day out, year after year. We offer them by way of sharing, learning together, and helping one another in our joint quest to do the best we can to meet our responsibility to the next generation.

Part I addresses aspects of personality development and the parents' and educators' role in it. Part II focuses on specific educational tasks and masteries. Part III deals with special concerns. They form a sequence, but each chapter also stands on its own, welcoming the interested reader.

Several of my co-workers have contributed to this book. They and many others who have participated in our joint undertakings have helped me to learn with them and from them over the years. Last, but certainly not least, this includes the parents and children. I thank them all most warmly.

Erna Furman

Acknowledgments

Chapter 1, "Play and Work in Early Childhood" (Erna Furman), was originally presented at the SPACE meeting of Rainbow, Babies and Children's Hospital, 1984, Cleveland; at the Annual Conference of the Ohio Association for the Education of Young Children, 1985, Cleveland; and at the Annual Workshop for Preschool Educators and Mental Health Professionals of the Cleveland Center for Research in Child Development, 1985, Cleveland. It was previously published in the Pamphlet Series of the Cleveland Center for Research in Child Development, 1985, and in *Child Analysis*, 1:60–76, 1990.

Chapter 2, "On Liking Oneself: Development of Self-esteem" (Erna Furman), was originally presented at the Annual Scientific Conference of Shady Lane School, 1986, Pittsburgh, and at the Annual Workshop for Preschool Educators and Mental Health Professionals of the Cleveland Center for Research in Child Development, 1987, Cleveland. It was previously published in the Pamphlet Series of the Cleveland Center for Research in Child Development, 1994.

Chapter 3, "On Preparation: 'New' Perspectives" (Robert A. Furman, M.D.), was originally presented at the Annual Workshop for Preschool Educators and Mental Health Professionals of the Cleveland Center for Research in Child Development, 1988, Cleveland. It was previously published in the Pamphlet Series of the Cleveland Center for Research in Child Development, 1988, and in *Child Analysis*, 1:26–41, 1990.

Chapter 4, "Helping Children Cope with Stress" (Robert A. Furman, M.D.), was originally presented at the Annual Workshop for Preschool Educators and Mental Health Professionals of the Cleveland Center for Research in Child Development, 1971, Cleveland. It was previously published in the Pamphlet Series of the Cleveland Center for Research in Child Development, 1994, and was published in *Young Children*, 50:33–41, January, 1995.

Chapter 5, "Working with Parents" (Ruth Hall), was originally presented at the Annual Workshop for Preschool Educators and Mental Health Professionals of the Cleveland Center for Research in Child Development, 1991, Cleveland. It was previously published in the Pamphlet Series of the Cleveland Center for Research in Child Development, 1991, and in *Child Analysis*, 4:62–74, 1993.

Chapter 6, "Thinking About Fathers" (Erna Furman), was previously published in *Young Children*, 47(4):36–37, May 1992, and in the *Newsletter of the Coalition for Fathers' Rights of Ohio*, October 1992, pp. 7–9.

Chapter 7, "Mothers, Toddlers, and Care" (Erna Furman), was originally presented at a Special Workshop of the Cleveland Center for Research in Child Development, 1984; at the 9th Annual Conference of the Michigan Association for Infant Mental Health, 1985, Ann Arbor; at the Forum for Mental Health Professionals of the North Carolina Psychoanalytic Society, 1987, Chapel Hill; and at several other scientific meetings. It was previously published in the Pamphlet Series of the Cleveland Center for Research in Child Development, 1984; by ERIC ED 256 479, Urbana, IL: University of Illinois at Urbana-Champaign; and in *The Course of Life: Psychoanalytic Contributions toward Understanding Personality Development*, Vol II, Early Childhood, ed. S. I. Greenspan & G. H. Pollock, Madison, CT: International Universities Press, 1989, pp. 61–82.

Chapter 8, "On Toilet Mastery" (Robert A. Furman, M.D.), was previously published in the Pamphlet Series of the Cleveland Center for Research in Child Development, 1991, and in *Child Analysis*, 2:98–110, 1991.

Chapter 9, "Plant a Potato: Learn About Life (and Death)" (Erna Furman), was originally presented at the Annual Workshop for Preschool Educators and Mental Health Professionals of the Cleveland Center for Research in Child Development, 1990, Cleveland. It was previously published in the Pamphlet Series of the Cleveland Center for Research in Child Development, in *CAEYC Review*, Spring 1987:1–4, and in *Young Children*, 46(1): 15–20, November 1990.

Chapter 10, "Learning to Enjoy Circle Time" (Erna Furman), was originally presented at the Annual Workshop for Preschool Educators and Mental Health Professionals of the

Cleveland Center for Research in Child Development, 1994, Cleveland. It was previously published in the Pamphlet Series of the Cleveland Center for Research in Child Development, 1994.

Chapter 11, "Where, When, and How to Go on Field Trips" (Yvette Anne Hoffman, in collaboration with Carol Eber, Erna Furman, Kate O'Rourke, Nancy Sabath, Barbara Welch), was previously published in the Pamphlet Series of the Cleveland Center for Research in Child Development, 1994, and has been submitted to *Young Children*.

Chapter 12, "Children in Hospitals—As Patients and Visitors" (Erna Furman), was originally presented at the Annual Workshop for Preschool Educators and Mental Health Professionals of the Cleveland Center for Research in Child Development, 1981, Cleveland. It was previously published in the Pamphlet Series of the Cleveland Center for Research in Child Development, 1981.

Chapter 13, "Sexual Abuse: Experiences with Prevention, Detection, and Treatment" (Erna Furman), was originally presented, in part, at the Annual Forum of the Cleveland Center for Research in Child Development, 1989, Cleveland, and previously published in *Child Analysis*, 4:113–129, 1993. The chapter also includes parts of an article titled "More Protections: Fewer Directions," which was previously published in *Young Children*, 42(5):5–7, July 1987, in *CAEYC Review*, Spring 1987:1–4, and in *Empathic Parenting*, 10(3):11–13, 1987.

Chapter 14, "Referring a Child for Special Help" I. "A Teacher's Role in Guiding Parents toward a Referral" (Luane Raia Lasky), was originally published in *CAEYC Review*, Spring 1975:10–16. II. "What Failures in Referral Have Taught Us" (Edward J. Schiff, M.D.), was originally presented at the Annual Workshop for Preschool Educators and Mental Health Professionals of the Cleveland Center for Research in Child Development, 1979, Cleveland, and previously published in *CAEYC Review*, Fall 1978:27–30. Both parts are included here with the kind permission of the Cleveland Association for the Education of Young Children and both are published in the Pamphlet Series of the Cleveland Center for Research in Child Development, 1994.

PART I

1

Play and Work in Early Childhood

ERNA FURMAN

Play and work are often linked, and just as often differentiated, in ways that are unhelpful to our understanding of them and, hence, to our ways of supporting children's development in both these areas. For example, many parents and professionals take the attitude of "play is the child's work." This may lead them to assume that children are working when they are really playing, or that their play will turn into the ability to work in the course of time, or that play can be a substitute for work—a mistake many a schoolchild, teacher, and parent discover too late, perhaps after years of games with words and numbers have not brought about the desired knowledge of spelling and multiplication tables which can be achieved only through the sustained effort and practice of work. Moreover, "play is the child's work" suggests that children play and adults work, a division that would impoverish the lives of both age groups. Actually, as I hope to show, play and work coexist from early on and make their separate and important contributions to our lives. The child's play and work may be simpler, the adult's more sophisticated, but all of us need to be able to play and work and are enriched by doing so.

Nevertheless, work and play often overlap and affect one another. A skill that was work to acquire may come to be used in the service of play; for example, learning to throw and catch a ball is work, but, with a sufficient level of skill, it may be used to play ball on one's own or in games with others, and it may even become work again for the professional ballplayer. With

3

some kinds of work, play is an essential preliminary; for example, playing with ideas, objects, or materials usually constitutes one stage in the work of the creative artist, scientist, and writer. Yet in other instances, play may turn into work (as when someone who likes playing with puppets becomes a professional puppeteer), or work may turn into play (as when a retired railway engineer likes to set up miniature railroads). However, none of these interactions or overlaps between play and work implies a maturational progression between them and the individual concerned usually senses some of the differences between working and playing in his own attitude, even when he enjoys both.

This brings us to another widely accepted but misleading attitude: "Play is fun; work is a hard chore." Writing on the pleasure in working, many years ago, I described how quickly young children sense our attitudes to work and how our daughter grappled with the question of whether work was fun, although one has to work to earn money. "For years my husband and I have attended a weekly professional meeting that takes place in the evening. Needless to say, our children never liked to see us leave for these meetings, but they accepted them as a part of the necessary work. On one such evening our four-year-old daughter told her babysitter, 'They always say they go there to work but I think they are having fun at the same time. Are these meetings for fun or are they work?' The sitter wisely refrained from answering this question and referred it to us. The next day we discussed with our little girl the fact that work is also fun and that work provides not only money but also pleasure. We told her that the difference between work and play was not that one was fun and the other wasn't.'' (E. Furman 1969a, p. 198). Rather, work and play make us feel good in different ways and yes, work has to be done even at times when it is not fun or is not fun right away. Pleasure in working depends in large measure not on the type of work but on the person doing it. Some people can find satisfaction even in the humblest routine tasks; others can never like their work, whatever it may be. This has a lot to do with our self-esteem, with the way we extend our liking, or not liking, of ourselves to our work, whether we can use our work to make us feel good, and how we were helped to develop our attitudes to work early on—a topic we shall return to.

The pleasures or satisfactions derived from work and play do differ but they also share an important characteristic. They never provide direct gratification of bodily needs, such as hunger, sleep, or elimination, or of impulses, sexual or aggressive. The pleasures of work and play are neither bodily nor instinctual. They are acquired tastes, acquired in the course of development and, like most other attributes, acquired with the help of the relationships with the parents at first and with teachers later.

Let us look at and compare some of the essential features of play and work, how they serve and enrich us, how they develop in early childhood, and how parents and teachers can assist children (E. Furman, 1992, 1993).

PLAY

Play always deals in symbols, that is, in things and activities we endow with meaning, so that they stand for something other than what they really are. With the help of these symbols play creates an imaginary world, a world of illusion, that mediates between ourselves and others. Almost anything can be used as a symbol in play—a utilitarian object (a chair becomes a pilot's seat), bodily gestures (the intently forward-leaning posture of the child sitting on that chair with his arms outstretched and hands clenched becomes the pilot grasping an imaginary steering wheel), noises (producing a ''whrrrr'' sound, the child suggests the revved-up engine); it can be lines and colors creating meaning in a painting or clay shapes in a sculpture; it can be toys, made to symbolize something but perhaps used to symbolize something else, such as the little plastic figure of a soldier who becomes a brave rescuer or a vicious terrorist; and, of course, the symbol used most often is words which themselves are symbols for things, ideas, and feelings.

The child's first plaything is what Winnicott (1953) called the transitional object. It is the infant's ''blankie'' or satin binding or soft toy or any other little handy thing the child uses to symbolize the space between mother and self and to create within this transition area a world of illusion that fills and bridges the gap. The transitional object usually includes a reminder of self and mother and of some interaction between them, but it also becomes a valued thing unto itself. It is the baby's first invention, the first product of his imagination, and its meaning is accepted and respected by both child and parent. We know how often mothers spend time and effort to make sure that this precious thing, which may in reality be a dirty, smelly rag, is taken along, is not washed lest it lose its special texture or smell, is searched for if lost, even if that involves driving a long way to where it may have been forgotten, and how mothers sympathize with the child's distress when he wants it and it is temporarily unavailable. The creation of the transitional object marks an important developmental step in the infant's life, dating usually to the latter half of the first year when mother and self have come to be experienced as separate people to an extent, when her absence is felt as the loss of an important person, and when interactions with her are conceived of as two people doing things to and with one another. Playing with the transitional object consists of and serves the same ends as all later play, albeit in a very rudimentary fashion. It satisfies, in an illusory way, what the infant wants to do to and with his mother and what he wants her to do to and with him when there is no real opportunity or possibility to achieve this interaction. Most often we think of the transitional object as a means of comfort, but it is much more, such as touching, mouthing, caressing, hurting, pinching, eating up and being eaten, being close and throwing away.

As the child grows older, he or she uses an increasing variety of things in play and gives them different and more varied special meanings. Some of the new playthings are toys; many others are household objects which, like the transitional object, derive their importance from the intimate interactions with the mother. What young toddler does not relish above all else to play with the contents of mother's kitchen cabinets, dresser drawers, and sewing basket? The transitional object usually becomes less often needed at this time, unless it begins to serve new purposes of play; for example, an early soft toy may come to be used as a more versatile complex doll. Not only the playthings, but the content of play itself begin to change. Through the use of pretend, playing increasingly satisfies many new, more advanced impulses and wishes, soothes new frustrations and disappointments, and gives meaning to the puzzles of life. Play draws on many inner and outer experiences, selects elements from them, blends them in new combinations, and brings them to new resolutions. Play never really changes the child or his world. The pilot's seat is still a chair and the pilot is still the same little boy when it is time to have lunch, but there has been a respite, perhaps an imagined gratification which helps to come to terms with reality, and most certainly there has been the special satisfaction that comes from creating something. Yes, the absorbed, intent and yet contained attitude, so characteristic of good play, reflects the fact that important business is going on.

It is important at the time and it is important for the future, because the young child's play of today helps to develop the imaginative resources on which we shall need to draw all our lives to symbolize our experiences, to give them meaning for ourselves and to share and understand the meaning others invent. This is essential to our continuing ability to enjoy playing on our own, with our children or pupils, and with other adults, however simple or sophisticated the game may be. It also enables us to invent and create, though perhaps only in a humble way—to tell or write a story, to draw a picture, to arrange a bouquet of flowers or to set a pleasing table, to decorate a cake or a corner in our home. It enables us to find beauty in our surroundings, in the patterns of the clouds and waves, in the dance of the leaves and the swoop of the birds, in the way the cat washes his face or the child skips along on the sidewalk. And of course it makes it possible for us to appreciate art, the imaginative creations of others in whatever form, and to participate in the cultural heritage of our community, all of which derives from mutually accepted beliefs and symbols to represent them. The child who cannot play cannot enter into and enjoy even the simplest story and will not learn to read to find pleasure in books, nor will he develop his own interests and hobbies. Instead, he will depend on being entertained by others or on being told what to do. Without inner resources, without play and all that it leads to, the quality of life is sadly diminished. We are left feeling empty and poor, regardless of how much money we may have.

WORK

In contrast to play, work always deals with reality and effects real results. Something, however humble, really gets done. The

sense of mastery and achievement that accompany the comple-
tion of work are its special pleasure and satisfaction. The process
of working, the effort expended on getting there, may also be
fun. Depending on the individual, almost every kind of work,
from the most humdrum routine task to the most complex under-
taking, may provide its own satisfactions. However, the process
of working usually also involves frustration and painstaking cor-
rection of mistakes, and it certainly involves waiting for the special pleasure in accomplishment. The baby who tries and tries to
handle his cup or to reach and hold on to his teething ring,
experiences the first beginnings of the process of working and,
when he succeeds, his beaming face tells us in no uncertain terms
that he knows the glow of accomplishment. This pleasure in
achieving a planned real goal is so great that it prompts us to
devote as much and more effort again and again to attain the
same results and to go on and try our hand at other tasks. It can
even sweeten the trying hurdles and setbacks along the way with
eager anticipation and spur us on, for one of the great advantages
of the pleasure in working and achieving is that it adds in a
lasting way to our self-esteem, to our confidence in ''I am a
somebody because I can do.'' This good feeling about ourselves
can only be acquired through working, through devoting effort
to achieve results. Even for the young child it can far surpass
the gratification of being catered to but remaining helpless and
undignified.

Unfortunately, not all of us realize our potential for gaining
pleasure from working and from using this pleasure to build our
self-esteem. We may not have had the opportunity or encouragement to persist and to achieve when we were growing up, to
taste the honey of hard-won accomplishment to please us and
our loved ones. So many things can get in the way and we need
so much of just the right kind of help. But those of us who do
enjoy working appreciate that it does more for us than earn a
living, though this alone is no minor accomplishment. Whereas
being able to play improves the quality of our lives, getting
satisfaction from work makes us feel that we are quality people.

HELPING CHILDREN WITH PLAY

The first and most crucial help toward the capacity to play is to
provide continuous and good enough mothering during the baby's first year, so that he can differentiate himself as a person

and view mother as separate from himself, with the first play and plaything naturally encompassing the space between them. Unfortunately, this development does not take place when there have been too many interferences, such as too much substitute or multiple care or too much dissatisfaction with need fulfillment or too much discomfort from illness or medical treatments. Some such children truly cannot play, cannot imagine, cannot use symbols. They can be told what to do, can often follow along with the play of others, but cannot initiate play and draw on their own resources. To help them in this area at a later time is almost impossible. Fortunately, most children do take these first developmental steps and their mothers value and respect their first toying.

It is of great help indeed when the caring adults extend this same value and respect to playthings and play at later stages. This attitude enables them to provide the conditions in which the child can develop his capacity for playing and in which play can contribute its proper share to personality growth.

In practice this implies protecting play from outside interference by allotting a safe space and sufficient time for playing. Children do not need a big space, a whole room or basement, much less the use of a whole floor. In fact, too large an area is distracting, except for large muscle activities. They need a contained niche or corner, away from the hot stove, the fragile nicknacks, the easily dislodged houseplants, not necessarily a place where toys are kept but one where a play-in-process can be preserved for later use or where a play product, such as a block building, can remain for a while to be relished by himself and admired by others. Above all, it has to be a place where the adult can keep an eye and ear on what is going on and can quickly step in when safety appears jeopardized. With the youngest children this often means that the best play corner is in the kitchen or living room, and that the child and his toys will inevitably tend to get under mother's feet.

Allowing enough time means recognizing that good play has a beginning, middle, and end, and needs to have a chance to be completed even though the end is not concretely marked by an achievement. How often we forget about this! How often we suddenly call a child away to some other task and expect him to interrupt himself because ''he's just playing,'' which means he is not doing anything important. We would not think of similarly

cutting short his schoolwork, much less his meal or sleep. Yet
with play, too, sudden interruption is not only frustrating and
disconcerting, but it makes it very difficult to resume later. When
children are interrupted often, they may not be able ever to regain
the peace of mind necessary to begin playing again. It is therefore
much more helpful to schedule enough time to start with or, if
there has to be an interruption, to give the child a few minutes'
warning in which he can reach an end or at least a stopping point.

Play also has to be protected from the interferences which
constantly threaten it from forces within the child. Since the
pleasures and satisfactions of play are always symbolic and imaginary, the young child's urgent bodily needs and as yet poorly
mastered excited and aggressive impulses tend to press for direct
gratification, break through into the play and engulf it. There is
a change in pitch. The little wooden hammer no longer hits the
pegboard but bashes the wall; the crayons are no longer used to
draw a picture but to scribble on hands and floor instead; the
pretend medical examination of teddy has shifted to investigating
the real bodily orifices of a peer or younger sibling; the playmate
arrested for an imaginary traffic violation is viciously wrestled
to the ground. At that point, the protests of "We were just playing!" and "He doesn't mind, he wanted me to!" ring hollow,
as do the thinly veiled rationalizations of "I was just getting a
spot off the wall" or "But that's the way they do it on the TV."
In truth, play has ceased to be play and turned into instinctual
discharge. At the time, the children's fun is so great that they
may object to the adult's interception, but in the long run they
appreciate that play was rescued—perhaps by being rechanneled
into the realm of illusion, or by being redirected, or even by
being stopped and a definite task being assigned instead to absorb
the excess energy. The least helpful approaches are not to interfere at all or to punish by demanding that the child sit still "to
think about it" with nothing to do. In the first case, the activity
will run its inevitable course to more and more trouble; in the
second, the generated tension will have no constructive outlet
and will burst forth in full force again at the next opportunity,
perhaps just after we have agreed to the apparently calm request,
"Can I now go play again?" The worst potential damage, however, is to play itself. As with repeated interferences from the
outside, repeated poorly managed interferences from inside the

child can, in a lasting way, jeopardize the ability to play alto-gether. Since there is no way to remove these potential inside intruders as one can with vases and hot stoves on the outside, and since children learn only gradually to master their needs and impulses in identification with their loved one's handling of them, their play needs the watchful caring adult's presence and availability to safeguard it. A stitch in time saves nine. A helpful reminder or assistance in effecting proper changes when the shift from symbolic containment to rising tension takes place is most helpful at the time as well as in the long run. It enables children to learn to gauge their own inner states and to participate actively in regaining their calmer equilibrium by figuring out ways of getting back to playing themselves.

Another area that demands the parent's or teacher's ever alert attention is the child's inner pressure to make play more real and to blur his still tenuous distinction between fantasy and reality. Often this shows in adding real elements to a play-in-process, for example, "Can we have some real raisins for our tea party?"—an appropriate touch of direct gratification which enhances the pleasure of play without disturbing it. At other times, however, reality may be disregarded to the detriment of play and of reality, for that matter. The use of real tools is usually unsafe; turning the living room upside down for a make-believe camp-out interferes with its use for the rest of the family and often damages the furniture; using mother's makeup and jewelry or dad's clothes from his drawers and closet as a rule oversteps the limits. Likewise, play can unhelpfully encroach upon the reality of time, for example, when the pretend cowboy fails to turn back into his true self at dinner or when playing goes on and on so as to interfere with getting ready for bed. In short, whenever children "get carried away with it," the grownup needs to help by being the guardian both of play and of the demands of the real world.

Parents and teachers, however, do not function merely as helping guardians; they are often needed to play with. Some important play proceeds, in Winnicott's (1958) words, "alone in the presence of someone," but this in itself is facilitated by the sufficient opportunity to play *with* someone, and this someone has to be the caring adult, at least in the earliest years and to some extent. This is a prerequisite, not a substitute, for play with peers. The latter, as we all know from experience, needs as much adult supervision as does play alone, if not more. When we offer, or are invited, to live for a while with our child or pupil in the shared world of illusion, both of us are enriched. It is a special pleasure to get to understand another's symbolic inner world and to find one's own understood and to find himself in one another, a way of being intimate without violating each other's space. For the child it is also a way of making his own the symbols of the family and community, which allows him increasingly to share in them. We may start with playing roll-a-ball and open the whole later world of games with balls that form such a big part of our culture pattern; we may start with making sand pies and pave the way toward creating and appreciating sculpture.

Yet even as pleasurable and important a thing as playing with our children and pupils has its caveat. We have to keep in mind that we are not only the playmate but also the caring adult. We must not get carried away ourselves by disregarding the rules of pretend, by introducing fantasy elements that frighten or overstimulate the child, by seemingly abrogating our role as the guardians of safety and reality, or by blurring fantasy and reality beyond the child's tolerance. This happens sometimes, for example when adults dress up on Halloween, or when a board or ball game gets too competitive.

In playing with our children we have fun, we share with one another as individuals, and we also transmit our cultural heritage. Toys are part of this heritage and indeed most traditional toys, such as dolls, puppets, balls, blocks, have proven themselves to be valuable play symbols over the centuries. But how many toys should a child have and what about all the new kinds of toys that flood the market in ever-increasing variety and technical sophistication? As to how many, we need to remind ourselves that a crowd of people does not necessarily give us a friend but can leave us bewildered and alone. Likewise, shelves full of toys may distract with their lifeless clutter, whereas a few beloved items may feel cozy and inviting. Many preschools and daycare centers have learned to keep some of their supplies stored away and to introduce never more than one new toy at a time, with several of its kind available to the group. And of course, the new toy, more often than not, requires a period of adult participation in playing with it, sometimes to help the child use it safely or to acquaint him with its potentials, but above all to add to it the ingredient of a pleasurable shared experience, that pinch of loving investment that makes the difference between the store-packaged meal and home cooking.

As to what kind of toys, we are constantly pressured to buy the latest product, temptingly advertised. The appeal to the child is pitched in terms of all the things the toy can do, how real and really gratifying it will be, like the doll that can drink and pass water, be made to walk and talk, and is clothed to be *the* baby or *the* teenager. The adults are promised all the things the toy will do for the child, keep him busy, meet his intellectual and emotional needs, help his motor skills, give him knowledge and know-how. When we do buy the toy, it is more often than not an initial thrill and a lasting disappointment, soon broken, lost or left in a forgotten corner. The reason is that good toys are not meant to do things *for* you, neither fulfill your needs and wishes nor teach you. Toys are good when you can do things with and for *them*, when their shapes and functions are vague enough to suggest versatile symbolic possibilities, to be fleshed out by the playing child's, not the toymaker's, imagination. The more specific the toy's features, the more it can do, the more it limits its use for the child and the more disappointing and crass is the realization of just how lifeless it is. Shakespeare's words required no theatrical props or scenery to delight his Elizabethan audiences, and the amorphous rag doll, perhaps lovingly made by a member of the family and certainly a part of shared play now and then, can be anybody and perform wonders much greater than the novelty status symbol toy with its rigidly circumscribed functions.

Clearly, playing is not an activity that gets young children off our hands or minds. "Go to your room and play so I can attend to other things" mostly sets the stage for good play soon to deteriorate or never to materialize at all. However, when we involve ourselves appropriately in our children's play during their early years, they will want and be able to play well on their own and with peers as they get older, will be able to use their resources in ever widening play-related areas, and will, in their turn, be able to enjoy helping their children with playing.

A child's difficulty with play may show itself in different forms, such as not being able to engage or be engaged in play at all, not being able to contribute to it with his own ideas, his play always becoming quickly engulfed by impulses or disregarding reality and its rules. Whatever the manifest interference, it may well point to serious personality trouble, but it may also relate to our not having helped enough in the right ways, and it may not be too late to start now.

HELPING CHILDREN WITH WORK

Work, like play, has its roots in the good-enough earliest mother-infant unit at the point when the child begins to differentiate himself from it. Whereas play initially fills and bridges the gap of separateness with imaginary interactions, the beginnings of work are linked to becoming like mother by doing what she does. Since, in the child's view, mother primarily does to him and for him, his first efforts are often expended on achieving the skill of doing for himself and show in his wish to feed himself. In the latter half of the first year, babies want to drink from a cup, hold their own bottle, put food and other things in their own mouth. They work at it with much energy and determination and enjoy their successes so much that this pleasure far outweighs that of being fed. Indeed, many of the eating disturbances that start at this time stem from babies not being allowed sufficient opportunity for weaning and self-feeding with mixed chewy food. We think of this as a step toward independence, but it implies learning to take over the mothering by doing as mother does. We see this in the infant's attempts to feed his teddy and often to feed mother, too.

If all goes well, the child's zest for "me do" soon grows by leaps and bounds and, throughout the toddler period, becomes his and mother's pleasure and bane. Youngsters muster surprising effort and perseverance at really doing all they see their loved ones do—turning on faucets, getting the telephone off the hook, climbing up to reach shelves. So often when they get into trouble it is hard to appreciate that they are really trying to be like us. And of course much of their "work" is neither welcome nor safe. But in the area of self-care the young child's motivated strivings find their most important and natural channels and deserve our full support. Every little step in self-feeding and serving himself, self-washing and drying himself off, self-dressing, getting out his clean clothes and putting the dirty ones into the wash, provides much scope for working and achieving successes that make him feel good, bring mother's approval, contribute to being a person in his own right, and build the confident self-esteem of "I can do." Toilet mastery as opposed to toilet training, an important distinction drawn by R. A. Furman (this volume, Chapter 8), is particularly helpful to the toddler in this respect, when he can want to become clean like the parents, can help dispose of the dirtied pants, flush the toilet, take part in washing himself off, get the clean clothes, learn to wipe himself and ultimately take pride in gauging his own body signals for elimination and use the toilet when he needs to. That is hard work for the child, takes many months and entails many setbacks and disappointments, but gives him a sense of achievement and a spur to tackle and master other tasks, quite different from the obedient submission to mother's toileting demands and ministrations. We are not left in doubt about that when we have had a chance to see two-year-old Mary proudly point out her bodily production in the toilet bowl, to watch Kevin's glowing face as he demonstrates putting on his coat after sliding his arms into it upside down in time-honored nursery tradition, or to hear Barbie's "me, all by myself" when she finally managed to slip into her new shoes after much struggling and twisting of feet. Work on self-care soon extends to caring for one's belongings, such as picking up toys, putting away clothes, and to helping the parents with the many tasks involved in meeting the family's needs and caring for house and home, such as cleaning, cooking, shopping.

None of this eases the parent's work. It is much quicker and more efficient to keep our youngster well away from all household chores and to continue our earlier full custodianship of his body care. Sometimes we even feel and act as though his functions were ours ("Eat a spoonful for Mommy," "Make in the potty now"), instead of recognizing that our role is to help him make them his own. We have to keep this very much in mind in assisting children with work toward self-care and work toward all other goals. Parents, and later teachers, need to be in tune with the child's ever-growing wish and ability to be his own person, to gauge which tasks or parts of tasks he can learn to master, to support his efforts with encouragement and admiration, to help overcome the frustration of mistakes and incompetence, and to share the pleasure in his accomplishments ("What a good spoon eater you are," "What a good face washer"). And when he can finally put on his jacket, wipe his behind, or carry his clothes to his room, we are still needed to stand by and admire and enjoy his mastery with him, because otherwise the accomplishment feels like it leads to the loved one's withdrawal instead of a new closeness through shared pleasure in working and achieving. One little girl expressed this well in words. She had experienced much difficulty with toileting because her mother had taken over control of her elimination, but then became clean rather quickly when mother could change to helping her daughter to participate actively. The mother was much relieved and, as soon as the little girl could take herself to the bathroom independently, she ceased to pay attention to the whole matter. A setback followed, with messes all over. When the mother inquired what had happened to the big girl who had so liked to be clean, her daughter explained, "But I can't go potty when you are not there. You have to wait for me in the hall outside the bathroom and then I don't need you." We are very much needed to establish the new satisfaction of achievement when we are no longer needed in the earlier ways.

During the preschool years the child can already build on the self-confidence and pleasure gained through previous work, has acquired more frustration tolerance, and is spurred on by his wish to be biggest and best and as grown-up as possible, which is so characteristic of this age group. The adult continues to help with supporting him to persevere through the hurdles of mistakes and failure and with being duly admiring of effort and achievement, but there are some new areas to work on as well. The preschooler's drive to be biggest, best, and most admired instantly, gets in the way of being realistic in assessing his own abilities and of tackling tasks that will not bring quick success or will not enable him to outshine others. This shows itself in many ways. Sometimes it leads youngsters to choose activities that are much too difficult or to set themselves goals that are much too high, which results in discouraging failures unless we assist them to make more appropriate choices and assure them of our trust that, step-by-step, they will advance toward the desired achievements. Many children judge their success or failure solely by comparison with others, and we have to redirect them toward comparing their work with their own past performance instead. If the child has tried his hardest and improved his performance even a little bit over the previous attempt, he can feel a sense of good achievement, even if others are better or worse at the same job. This goes parallel with learning to appreciate that some things are harder or easier for different people and that we may be good at different things. It is also important that we be realistic and discriminating in our praise, expecting just a bit more effort and time to be devoted to the work each time, so that admiration does not become automatic, but deserved and worth working for. It helps even more to withhold our assessment at first and to encourage the child to assess his achievement himself. Sometimes he may find he has indeed done a good job and we can support his proud look back at his own work. The self-esteem gained from justified good self-assessment counts for more than the mere recognition by others. Sometimes, of course, self-assessment leads to justified self-criticism, and then the child needs help to correct his mistakes or to try again harder or to learn a step he had not understood. More often than not, however, children do not assess their work realistically, exaggerate its merits or underestimate its worth, and that is when they need our opinion most to become more realistic with themselves. Sometimes preschoolers are so afraid of not achieving well, or of not achieving as well as others, or of tolerating the disappointment of mistakes, that they just quietly avoid certain activities or make up excuses for not working at them. Helpful parents and educators watch out for this, encourage the child to try his hand at these neglected tasks or even make them part of an assignment. The child's self-doubts may prove to be imaginary or he may indeed need extra help. In either case, lack of practice can only lead to falling behind and to feeling even less good about himself. Really trying, really working, even before a goal is achieved, needs to be valued and praised and bear the mark of achievement for its own sake. No child learns this without adult help.

The ability to work and to enjoy work comes largely through identification with the loved ones' attitudes to their work. If he sees them not only encouraging and liking his working but taking pleasure in working and achieving themselves, he is most likely to make that attitude a part of his own personality. We have to keep in mind, however, that the young child primarily observes us at work with the daily manual chores that keep the household going and provide for the family's basic needs. Whether and how much we may enjoy our work as professionals or at the office or factory matters less to him than how we go about the routine tasks of cooking and washing, of shopping and taking care of the yard. Even when he observes our work as teachers in the preschool, what counts most is not our skill at preparing the right educational material, but how we mop up after a spill or how we go about putting on boots or putting away blocks. If we can take pride in doing these jobs well and if we can let our children help us with them, even if it takes longer, there will be the special pleasure of working together and of shared accomplishment. When children do not want to do chores, it is often because the adults did not like doing those chores and handed them on as tasks that they considered neither satisfying nor worthwhile. It is quite different to be allowed to take over a job that the grownups really rather liked and are just a little reluctant to give up.

The later satisfactions from more sophisticated work rest on and grow out of the early self-esteem of ''I can do, I can achieve, I am a somebody'' which we help our children and pupils acquire through our example and through our support of their efforts to master the basic tasks that make up their daily life.

2

On Liking Oneself

ERNA FURMAN

All of us who care for or work with young children want them to like themselves, to feel good about themselves. In part, our wish is altruistic. We want the best for them because we like them and care about them. In part, our wish stems from wanting them to do well—be cooperative and kind with people, zestful and patient in learning, self-controlled and self-protective in behavior. We know that such "doing well" is most effectively motivated, not by seeking praise or fearing punishment, but by thinking well of themselves and always wanting to preserve, enhance, or regain that good feeling.

Liking oneself is not a given. It is acquired step by step, at first mostly with the help of the caring adults, later increasingly through one's own often painstaking efforts, with preschool educators contributing their own share as teachers and as mother substitutes. Getting a good early start on liking oneself is so important that it is well worth a concerted effort in helping your youngsters with it and helping them to help themselves. A solid foundation laid during their preschool years will stand them in good stead lifelong; without it, later efforts will be much harder and achievements will be shaky at best.

Of the many things that build our basic self-regard, our feeling good about ourselves, we shall touch on three crucial areas—liking one's bodily self, liking to do and master, and being on good terms with one's conscience.

LIKING ONE'S BODILY SELF

The First "Me"

During the first few months of life, a baby's good experiences become the basis of his concept of "me." Good means pleasurable but not too intense, and it is hoped good experiences are those of the body—eating, sucking, digesting, eliminating, being safely held, gently cleansed. Feeling good prompts the baby to seek out and repeat these experiences and helps him to get to know, like, and own parts of his body.

At the same time, wanting to feel good leads him to protest pain and discomfort and to avoid chewing, biting, or scratching himself, i.e., the self-hurting activities often manifest in newborns but usually already avoided in the latter half of the first year. These are crucial steps in the psychological development of the personality and in its capacity for survival and self-preservation. They are not physiological givens at birth, nor do they mature on their own. They come about through consistent empathic care by the mothering person, a fact the baby soon comes to appreciate. He connects his good experiences with her presence and learns that her soothing ministrations can do away with discomfort and restore his good feeling. We take it as a hallmark of normal development when the older baby recognizes his mother and protests her leaving and when, if hurt or in pain, he seeks her out and accepts her comforting. This achievement is the point at which the earlier good experiences have succeeded in forming the core of a bodily "me" that likes itself enough to be motivated to do well by itself and to enlist the help of others for this purpose when necessary. Nothing could be more important for our future ability to care well for our bodily health and to stand as a lifelong inner protection against self-inflicted harm. It is sad and dangerous indeed when a baby cannot achieve this stage, either because his mother could not provide sufficient good experiences or, in the case of illness, could not soothe enough. But, important though these first achievements are, they need to be stabilized and extended during the next years.

How Toddlers Learn to Like Their Bodies

The toddler phase is particularly important for learning to like and be kind to one's body and, as earlier, this depends largely on the relationship with the primary mothering person. The older infant and young toddler have come to appreciate that their well-being hinges on her availability, that she is not an ever-present part of them, and that they are vulnerable without her. Looking out for signs that she might leave and protesting when she does leave are healthy indications of self-protectiveness. If separations are not too frequent or too long, if they are prepared for and mother herself assures her child that she is handing him over to a familiar trusted substitute who will carry out her caring and protective function at her behest until her return, he can be helped to cope and maintain his newly won self-protectiveness.

Older youngsters often show that by insisting that the sitter do for them exactly as mother does. Younger ones often simply refuse to cooperate and/or become very distressed and will not eat, sleep, or get dressed when the sitter cannot or does not know how to approximate mother's handling. By contrast, the youngster who does not protest mother's leaving, readily accepts any caregiver, and does not mind when his needs are met and his body cared for in different ways, shows us that he has either not developed a phase-appropriate self-protectiveness or has lost it under the impact of separation. It is not a sign of mature adaptability, often welcomed by the adults, but an important signal of normal development being endangered. Young toddlers placed in daycare often lose their self-protectiveness to the point of not protesting pain and not seeking and accepting comfort, with injuries and illness going unnoticed even by attentive caregivers because the child does not alert them to his discomfort (see this volume, Chapter 7). Sometimes the child recaptures his self-protectiveness on reunion with his mother, crying and showing her what hurts; sometimes even reunion fails to bring back the lost ability.

It is not mother's mere presence that matters, however. It is her attitude, her loving, respectful care and consideration of his body, which make him feel good and which he, step-by-step, internalizes as his attitude to himself. This is not an easy task for any mother when her toddler is no longer a compliant baby who sleeps long hours, but is now a zestful toddler, running all over the place, wanting to hold everything in his daily widening range, and asserting his own likes and dislikes over his bodily needs—be it what he will eat, when he will sleep, or whether or not he will eliminate. It makes mothers impatient, angry, and worried. It tempts them to get rough, intrusive, forceful, even to hurt their child's body, forgetting that their treatment of him will not only become the way he treats others but, above all, the way he will treat his own body.

What makes it especially hard for mother and child during the toddler phase is that they are still in many ways part of one another, struggling to become and to view each other as separate persons and to delineate the boundaries between them. When Johnny won't eat his breakfast, it is hard for mother to appreciate that he may not be hungry or may not need certain foods just now because she still experiences his need as her own and is therefore convinced that she knows when he is hungry and knows what his body is hungry for. In parallel fashion, Johnny may still confuse himself with mother and, sensing how much it matters to her, may well refuse to eat ''for mommy'' to tease or punish her, forgetting that it is he, not mommy, who will then go hungry. Similarly, when Johnny runs into the street, mother may experience it as a threat to her own safety and punish him for scaring her, and he, reciprocally, may tease her by doing it, oblivious to the fact that the harm would come to him. Courting danger or hurting oneself to distress another does not lead to self-protectiveness.

It is so helpful when mother can catch herself, realize their separateness, and assist her toddler with it. Then, at breakfast, she will not have to convince him or feel offended and angry at his not eating, will not have to nag, spoon-feed, or threaten him, but will just be able to tell him matter-of-factly, ''I guess you aren't hungry now and perhaps you'll be hungry by snacktime, but *I* am hungry and don't want to wait till snacktime, so I'll eat my breakfast now.'' And with his tendency to dash into the street, she will make sure that she keeps her eyes and hand on him to prevent it and, when he tries to pull away from her, will just say, ''No, I won't let you because the street is not safe. *You* could be hurt.''

Youngsters will need constant and vigilant protection throughout the preschool years, but by the age of three they have, with good help, extended their own self-protectiveness to avoiding common dangers, i.e., dangers commonly encountered in their familiar environment, such as hot stoves, electric outlets, moving objects, and street traffic. As mother stresses that being safe is an important part of her caring, this becomes a valued part of the child's own self, of his body and its space.

Building on the infant's limited sense of a bodily "me," the toddler extends his bodily self-concept to include all the body parts he sees and feels. This encompasses his face which he can only see in a mirror but can feel with his hands, and his behind which he can never see but learns to feel, especially with the help of eliminating and learning to wipe himself. At the same time, he comes to differentiate and appreciate many inside parts of his bodily "me," the sensations that alert him to his needs and impulses and the good feelings that come with satisfying each.

The Preschooler's Bodily Concept

During the preschool years, all the toddlerhood gains in owning, liking, and taking good care of one's body are continued and extended. A special task of this period is to include one's sexual organs as a liked and valued part of oneself and to understand and accept the differences between boys and girls as well as between child and adult. Here again, the parents' attitudes and their relationship with the child are very important. Their help does not lie in demonstrating the differences, in showing the child who has what or can do what, but rather in valuing the child for what he is (boy or girl) and valuing the spouse's as well as one's own sex. Parents help likewise by listening for and answering their child's questions and clarifying his or her misunderstandings, such as the common assumption that the visible external attributes constitute one's sexual organs and, consequently, divide people into haves and have-nots. At best, there are ups and downs as youngsters struggle to comprehend, to cope with feelings of envy and/or inferiority, and to come to terms in such a way that they not only know and accept their gender, but like what they are. Parents who are in tune with their child will be alert to his or her questions and empathic with the related feelings. They will also know that both questions and feelings are often conveyed by a look or piece of behavior, rather than through words.

Early sexual knowledge and feelings—like later sexual behavior in our society—are primarily a private family matter, best addressed in the home between parents and children. In preschool and daycare, however, there are often opportunities to observe the direct and indirect manifestations of a child's concerns. It is most helpful to share such observations with the parents so that they can help at home as well as to discuss with them ways in which the school or center can assist them and their child (E. Furman, 1986a).

ME ALL BY MYSELF

As adults we realize that doing things well and accomplishing difficult tasks makes us feel good, even proud of ourselves. But, unless we become incapacitated through illness or injury, we are not aware how much self-regard and self-esteem we derive from functioning as self-sufficient individuals in daily living—being able to feed, toilet, clean, and dress ourselves, being able to walk, run, exercise, do things with our hands, get places on our own. The toddler, not unlike a severely handicapped invalid, is help-less, dependent on the availability and good will of others to do for him. To the functioning adult, being served and done for may at times seem very gratifying, but to the toddler and invalid being able to do for oneself is the most desirable state, the very condition for being a somebody.

The Role of Self-care

Bodily self-care is the first and most important vehicle toward becoming an independent "I can do" person in one's own right, one for whom doing and mastering is an ongoing source of liking and valuing oneself. "Me do" is the healthy toddler's constant demand of self-assertion and "me all by myself" is the glowing acme of self-esteem through achievement.

Young toddlers' intense admiration as well as envy of moth-er's caring and need-fulfilling activities prompt him early on to want to take them over and make them a part of himself. Feeding, washing, dressing oneself, going to sleep on one's own, becom-ing clean and in charge of one's toileting, all are difficult skills to learn and, at best, take much time and effort to master. What makes the process even harder is that the toddler wants to do them on his own right away while the mother is partly reluctant to hand them over to him—not only because she can do it so much more efficiently and quickly, but also because doing for her little one is a special source of gratification for her. When the relationship between them is consistent and good enough, they have a chance of working it out and taking a big step toward a new kind of relationship, from being part of one another to being separate loved and loving individuals.

The process of acquiring bodily self-care, paralleled by mother handing over bodily care, goes through four interrelated stages. The first is "doing for" which is where mother and baby start, although the in-tune mother watches for and allows her infant's active participation, be it waiting for his readiness to nurse or letting him hold a washcloth during bathing. The second stage is "doing with," where, bit by bit, the older infant and young toddler do more and more of their own caretaking, with mother assisting or completing the task. The child's uncooperativeness with any part of the joint effort usually and healthily signals that he is ready to do more as well as that he trusts mother to respect and support his wish. When he screams or turns away his face at her wiping his mouth, he is ready to work at wiping it himself; when he splashes in the tub or throws out his bath toys, he wants to work at washing and even drying off himself; when he squirms on the changing table, he is eager to stand up and help with cleaning himself. Eventually one or another part of self-care is mastered sufficiently for the child to do it on his own. This ushers in the most crucial third stage of "standing by to admire." It is the time when mother is not needed for doing or teaching how to do, but for handing over her loving enjoyment of her child's bodily care. As she watches, admires, and appreciates his doing for himself, she conveys to her youngster that very loving investment which will make self-care a permanent source of his self-regard. The skills alone do not carry that liking of oneself. Without mother's available love of them to use as one's own, they can be mere chores, easily given up under stress or angrily used to spite. Likewise, self-care skills learned from others (siblings, relatives, sitters, daycare caregivers) do not become stable valued parts of the self and do not serve in the same way as a source of liking oneself (E. Furman, 1993).

Mothers rarely appreciate how much they are needed when they just stand by to admire and how much their doing so is a prerequisite for the fourth and last stage, namely, "doing by oneself" and feeling good because of it. Owning one's bodily needs and related bodily parts and being able to take care of them are the matrix of liking oneself, the foundation in which self-regard stemming from the concept of the bodily self and self-regard stemming from doing and mastering come together. Without that foundation other pleasures in functioning and achieving are, at best, diminished, and at worst, unattainable. Many youngsters who shine by knowing their letters, numbers, and colors, or by coloring in pictures, derive little inner self-esteem from these accomplishments when they still do not know how to wipe their own behinds or how to put on their boots and jackets.

The Role of Personality Functions

Beyond bodily self-care, however, and usually concurrently with it, self-regard comes from other forms of doing which also develop during the toddler phase and preschool years and which also use the four-stage process of interaction with the parents to become a valued part of the self. These include motor control of large and small muscles, speech, memory, perception, and making sense of what one perceives, i.e., understanding reality, and thinking to figure things out for oneself and to interpose as mental trial before acting.

Parents are constantly reminded how important it is to stand on one's own feet, literally and figuratively, when their toddler protests being picked up and carried and even refuses to hold hands. They need to steer carefully between respecting their child's wishes on the one hand and guarding his safety as well as being ever so patient on the other hand. Although some of the personality functions develop spontaneously with maturation, all of them need the careful transition from doing for, to doing with, to standing by to admire, before they can be a source of self-esteem as an integrated part of the personality. It is not easy to allow time and give careful supervision for learning to go up and down the stairs when there are so many chores waiting to be done; not easy to listen to the child's hard-to-understand words and mixed-up ideas instead of just telling him what's what; not easy to praise him for being a good "looker" and "rememberer" when he sees, hears, and remembers things we would prefer he had forgotten or not noticed in the first place; not easy not to laugh at his mixups of animate and inanimate, fantasy and reality, but to clarify instead. Yet most parents are sufficiently in tune with their youngster to appreciate how much each of his growing mental functions needs safe scope, time, loving investment, and admiration that they are willing to support its development, despite the inconvenience and annoyance at times, and, instead of getting angry, praise his efforts and achievements.

Recognizing, owning, tolerating, and naming one's feelings is as important, if not more so, than other functions. And parental help is especially crucial in assisting the child with the transition from bodily sensations and motoric discharge to mentally experienced differentiated feelings. When the infant is upset or overstimulated he responds with eating troubles, digestive upsets, or sleep interferences. The upset or overstimulated toddler tends to respond with motoric discharge, becoming hyperactive, running around excitedly or touching and doing all the wrong things. Recognizing these inner signals as feelings and learning to express them in words helps him to know when he is happy, sad, angry, scared. This not only stops burdening his bodily needs and calms his behavior. More important, feelings alert us to figuring out the situation that causes them and what we can do about it. They are an indispensable inner prompter to effective thinking and doing. When a child knows he is angry (and neither tummy aches nor misbehavior help him know he is angry), he can more readily figure out who or what makes him angry and address the source.

Many a toddler who has trouble going to sleep or trouble being demanding and contrary has been greatly helped by mother pointing out that perhaps not letting her go at bedtime and bossing or disobeying her comes from feeling angry at her. As he came to know and express his anger in words, they could then figure out its cause, perhaps mommy's leavings. This made the leavings themselves harder, but it freed up the interferences with sleeping and misbehavior and it made it possible to find ways of mitigating the stress of separation. Sometimes telephone calls helped, sometimes keeping something of mommy's, sometimes having a "missing mommy box" which the child filled with items to remind him of mommy or with toys he wanted to play with during her absense. Whatever plan they worked out, it made the hard feelings more tolerable and made more loving and being loved available to tame the anger.

When parents help with and value owning feelings, then knowing, using, containing them become a sure source of feeling in charge of oneself and liking oneself as part of the "I can do." Being out of control is never a source of self-esteem, even when the immediate discharge provides some gratification of angry or excited impulses.

Mastering Difficult Tasks

The most advanced source of self-esteem through doing and mastering is the one we know best as adults, namely, working at and achieving what comes hard. This is already very much a part of acquiring self-care and pleasure in functioning, but also extends to learning various skills and pursuing activities that provide no immediate gratification of bodily needs or impulses. Working hard at something may even require giving up some such satisfactions, for example, when learning to like oneself to be clean and kind demands foregoing the earlier impulses of liking to mess and enjoying being mean or cruel. And with some skills, such as sewing or doing puzzles, impulse gratification would be an interference. What is always involved, however, is the learning and valuing of frustration tolerance, the coping with the ubiquitous restrictions of "not here but there," "not now but later," "not this but that."

Frustration tolerance is not a given and does not mature spontaneously. It is acquired in part by identification with the loved parents' model and in part through their supporting, valuing, and praising the child's efforts toward it. Valuing the ultimate achievement is important as it becomes a source of shared pleasure and paves the way for the separate own pleasure. But often it is even more important to value each little step of the difficult process of getting there. The fact that he still messed in his pants may not be as important as the fact that he tried to alert mother and tried to get to the potty and tried to pull down his own pants. Likewise, the finished puzzle may not be as important as his persistence and patience in fitting in piece after piece, not giving up when it did not fit, and keeping on trying. One almost three-year-old had worked at his sewing card for a long time. He did not finish it, but as he stored it away, planning to work at it again the next day, he said, "Now I am a good tryer."

PARENTS' AND TEACHERS' SELF-ESTEEM

As parents and preschool educators we too need to take progressive steps and learn to value new things in ourselves. It comes quite naturally to feel at one with the very young child and therefore to experience his successes as our own or, at other times, his failures as a reflection on ourselves. The children sense this attitude keenly and, with justification, experience it as a diminishment of themselves. Valuing his toilet cleanliness because it shows us up as a good mother (and is less trouble) or valuing his nice picture because it shows us up as a good teacher, leaves no room for helping the child to value himself through his own accomplishments. We have to make a consistent effort to let him have his own successes and failures and to derive our self-esteem from supporting his owning them—something like "I like myself when I help him to take over." In time, we may derive a special pleasure from his doing his things in the way we did them for and with him. He is becoming like us. Sometimes there is a special pleasure in his doing things of his own choice and in a different way. Perhaps he identified with our individualistic self-initiative. Even when we cannot trace anything of his to something that perpetuates a piece of ourselves, our self-esteem can rise with the thought, "I helped him to become his own person and to like himself."

BEING ON GOOD TERMS WITH ONE'S CONSCIENCE

The Role of the Parents

The area where young children take in parts of ourselves most readily is the area where we often notice it the least—the do's and don't's, the rights and wrongs, what is good and what is bad. The hundreds of daily praises and prohibitions that convey our values and standards seem so often disregarded or disobeyed that we do not always appreciate how much and how early they become lodged within the child's own mind and ultimately form his conscience. Having a ''good conscience'' can mean that our conscience is pleased with us and likes us. It can also mean that it is a conscience that is a consistent, helpful guide to doing the right things, alerting us to potential wrongdoing beforehand and, if we fail, alerting us through guilt to the need to correct or make up for what we did wrong. In both senses of the phrase it means having a helpful parent inside. Indeed, in many ways our conscience is the inner representative of the way we perceived our external parents during our earliest years. To be on good terms with our conscience, to trust that it will always be there to like us when we do right, to admonish us not to do wrong, and to help us put it right if we fail, is as crucial to our mental well-being throughout life as having that kind of parents was to our well-being in early childhood. A good conscience, like a good parent, demands neither too much nor too little, does so consistently, focuses on prevention, and relies on the rewards of loving approval and on making amends to dispel disapproval.

Parents are often unaware of the tremendous power they exercise by virtue of their mere approval. To be liked and approved of by one's parents, the most important and the most needed people in the whole world, is the most wonderful feeling. It prompts loving and admiration and with it the wish to become like them, and that is the very vehicle by which parental values and standards are best taken in and made one's own. Approval renders disapproval so uncomfortable that every effort is made to prevent it or to regain approval—not unlike the way feeling good bodily becomes an inner guardian against incurring pain and, at times of pain, prompts us to do something about it that will restore the good feeling.

Harsh anger and punishments are also taken in, but they convey and arouse so much negative feeling that they cannot be absorbed and therefore cannot serve as a helpful inner guide. Instead, they may turn into mental tormentors, preventing inner harmony and self-esteem, or, to get rid of them, may have to be turned outward and result in critical or punitive interactions with others. In a way, it is like with food: good food is well digested and readily contributes to bodily growth; bad food cannot be digested, causes tummy troubles, may have to be expelled, and does not further growth. Most parents realize that harsh anger and punishments "do not really work" and are, most often, an expression of their, the parents', angry, impatient exasperation. They wish they had done or could do differently, just like their children often wish that for themselves.

Of course, we all are most likely to get angry when we *know* that the child *knows* the right things to do. But if he knows, why is he so obstreperous and disobedient? Why does he not heed our warnings? Why does he flaunt the rules so frequently? The child's trouble is not with not knowing right from wrong, but with not having the personality means to behave accordingly. Wishes and impulses are strong when self-control is still minimal. Under these circumstances, the demands of inside rules are easily overridden and may only reassert themselves after wrongdoing, perhaps in the form of guilt, fear, or feelings of inadequacy. For this reason, acquiring a helpful conscience goes hand in hand with acquiring tools of mastery. Both depend on the parents' ability to negotiate with their child the successive steps of doing for, doing with, and standing by to admire, before the "doing by oneself" phase is reached. For some things, such as not biting people, this last phase is reached during toddlerhood; for other things, such as not letting oneself be swayed by the behavior of others, it may not be reached till late adolescence. Throughout these many years children have ample opportunity to observe (and to observe very astutely!) whether the adults practice what they preach. Insofar as they do, their message will be unequivocal and will be internalized as such. If they do not, their double standards will become the child's own. This "Do as I say, but not as I do" approach may show in such simple matters as hitting the child but forbidding him to hit others who are smaller and weaker, or in subtler ways, such as forbidding him to lie while the parent cheats on traffic rules or income tax.

Conscience Development in Toddlerhood

Toddlers are so zestful and so lacking in self-control that parental "don't's," uttered in panic or anger, easily proliferate, leaving little room for praise for doing things right. It helps to remember that the parents still have to function for the toddler when it comes to preventing wrongdoing. Even with constant supervision, they need to be ever ready to help find ways of making amends when prevention has not worked—be it helping clean up a spill, putting back what was taken off a shelf, or returning a toy snatched from a peer. Prevention and making up are especially important at this stage because the parental ''don't'' has already been taken in, usually in a much more threatening form than intended, and the more so the less it can as yet affect the child's behavior. We can observe this in many a toddler's angrily distorted face and shaking finger as he stands in front of a precious item, perhaps even saying ''no, no'' just before he grabs it. We see it also in the ways toddlers misinterpret events as punishment for past wrongdoings. For example, when little Janie got ill with yet another respiratory infection and her mother mused, ''I wonder how you got that cold,'' Janie quickly replied, ''Jumping on mommy-daddy bed.'' Likewise, youngsters often assume that they are put in daycare or left with a sitter because they had been bad, although such punishment was never articulated or executed. At best, toddlers' knowledge of right and wrong has some chance of asserting itself helpfully *only* in the mothering person's presence. This gives her a chance to spot the moment's delay or questioning look before wrongdoing and, while helping with prevention, to praise her child's knowing and to underline how good it will feel to do the right thing, ''So grown-up, just like mommy and daddy.''

During the toddler phase, learning to like oneself as clean and as kind are among the most important values a child acquires in identification with his parents. Since young toddlers like being dirty and often enjoy hurting others' bodies, feelings, or possessions, these new values are hard to come by. Mothers support them by being clean and kind themselves, by pointing out how good they feel when they are clean and kind and would not like themselves to be dirty or mean, by preventing their toddlers from indulging in messing and hurting, by enlisting them in cleanup and makeup, by valuing every little sign of the child's effort at being clean or kind. Independent toilet mastery may be the ultimate achievement in being clean, but even not liking dirt on one's fingers is a praiseworthy first step. Likewise, keeping one's good feelings for mommy and taming one's anger at her when she frustrates or disappoints may be the ultimate achievement in kindness, but even picking up a dropped item for her is a praiseworthy first step.

Supporting the Preschooler's Conscience

The transition from toddler to preschooler is gradual, but there usually comes a moment when mothers give a sigh of relief, realizing that they spend much less time and effort running after their child, can trust him for a little while in the other room even as they listen, and, when the suspicious noise or silence warrants intervention, they can talk to their child first instead of having to dash there, because now verbal contact will often serve as a reminder to keep in control. This and many other signs show us that the preschooler has much better inner controls and increasingly uses them to live up to his inner expectations. He can even use them better without mother's presence and when in the care of others, which makes it possible for him to adapt to a preschool setting.

It is still very important for the preschooler to know that his home standards either are the same as those of his teacher or, if not, that mother knows about the difference and has agreed to it. Time and again, children feel very conflicted when they are encouraged to use paint or water at preschool if these activities are not permitted in the home setting. They may refuse, not giving in to temptation, or they may have a great time with it but then feel bad and act up at home to provoke punishment without ever confessing their "sin." Obversely, children who are used to physical punishment often think that the lack of it at preschool means that there anything goes. This may tempt them to misbehave at school as well as at home, the former by way of indulgence, the latter by way of seeking punishment. It helps so much when parent, teacher, and child can discuss differences in standards and/or consequences for not living up to them, and to assure the child that the parent endorses the variant.

Conscience, its values, expectations, and punishments, derive from the relationship with the parents. During the later school years and adolescence, teachers and others contribute to the widening and modification of a child's conscience, but during the early years teachers, caregivers, and even members of the wider family do not contribute. Their important role lies in making sure that the parental standards hold while the child is in their care and that they assist him in living up to them by reminding him of them and by working on the many means of self-control he needs to achieve them. The consistency of standards, including parentally permitted variations, not only avoids temptation and undue guilt. It also helps to build a consistent conscience, one that will stand by the child later when he finds himself in new situations or groups where "doing as others do" would lead him astray.

Preschoolers may need less supervision and "doing for" than toddlers, but they need a lot of "doing with" and of "standing by to admire" in the area of conscience. They often alert us to their as yet insufficient ability to modify their behavior and to their qualms about it. At this age, tattling and criticizing or admonishing others are not a sign of unkindness but a signal of inner conflict about their own wrongdoing. Henry would so consistently inform me about peers' naughtiness that I could safely respond with, "Henry, I think you want me to know that *you* did something you feel bad about. Perhaps you can tell me just what it was and then we'll figure out how you can put it right." Henry's confession would follow promptly. We could then discuss whether he would think it best to make a picture or an apology note for the child he had hit, or whether rebuilding was in order for the boy whose block structure he had knocked over, or whether it would help him feel good again if he offered to accept into his game the girl he had unkindly rejected. My repeated "*Soon* you will try to stop yourself before and like yourself doing it just right" did not materialize *soon*, but it helped Henry increasingly to listen to his conscience and to value its loving approval when he could make amends—important steps along the way. Increasingly, too, I noticed Henry doing spontaneous acts of kindness, such as helping me or a peer, and I tried not to miss these moments to point out how thoughtful he was and how pleased he could be with himself.

The Kindergartener's Conscience

Five- and six-year olds take a big step in conscience formation. Sometimes the change is so sudden and so big that it seems strange to them to hear that "inside" voice, especially as it is often so harsh and demanding. Even adults may experience their conscience as "I hear my mother telling me." But it is not always experienced as the parent's voice and is readily attributed to other adult authorities, in part because it feels safer to locate it outside oneself where one has a chance of hiding from it. For the kindergarten teacher, helping children with their conscience is an ongoing task. The unfamiliar yet ever-present inner monitor needs the adults' help to become recognized appropriately. It often needs help to distinguish big, medium, and little wrongdo-ings (because it tends to view all as major crimes!), and it needs help with being experienced as a loving inner friend when we do well, as well as with changing from a tyrant to a guide that is realistically reproachful and forgiving after amends have been made.

How often children tell at home how mean their teacher is, how critical and demanding! How often they fear the principal as though he were the last judgment! And how often it helps when parents and child can meet with the teacher and trace her "meanness" back to the child's exaggerated self-criticism, or when the teacher finds an opportunity in class to clarify that the child's protest at her expectations comes from his own expecta-tion of perfect worksheets, while she expects mistakes and merely views them as a chance to learn more.

But youngsters fear other things too—illness, death, mon-sters, robbers—all the agents of punishment for unatoned guilts which become especially threatening at night when they are alone with their conscience. And here again it helps when the parents can understand and even trace the guilts that make for sleep-time fears—the unfinished assignment, the poor grade on a test, the school crayons appropriated and now hiding in the drawer, or the unkindness to a friend perpetrated in anger. Then ways can be found to correct the wrongdoing and to be forgiven as well as to forgive oneself, and unrealistic demons are laid to rest.

Some children find it so hard to listen to and live with their new conscience that they may act as though they did not have one. They become unruly and mischievous. Parents and teachers are apt to say, "He's asking for it" and, in a way, that describes it correctly, for the child provokes punishment from outside in preference to the usually much harsher punishment that threatens him from inside. When kindergarteners, and even first graders, indulge in wrongdoing, we can pretty much take it for granted that they are not *using* their conscience, rather than that they do not have one. Reminding them of their conscience is therefore more important than telling them what to do, and reminding them when and how their conscience can make them feel good about themselves is at least as important as pointing out when it makes them feel bad. "Remember how good you felt yesterday when you managed recess so well? I bet you that good feeling will help you try very hard again today so you can feel just as good about yourself. You just keep a very good eye on yourself and come and tell me how it worked for you."

Liking our body, liking to do and to master, and feeling liked by our conscience make up most of our self-regard and self-esteem. One hopes that this liking of oneself and the help one got with it all through the years are realistic. This means being able to recognize and appreciate the good, to note and tolerate the bad, and to do one's best to make the bad better. But it also implies accepting one's lack of perfection and the fact that others may be better than we are in one or another area.

3

On Preparation: "New" Perspectives

ROBERT A. FURMAN, M.D.

Some of Freud's discoveries during the first world war are absolutely fundamental to understanding what preparation is all about. At that time Freud (1920, p. 31) tried to figure out what had transpired in the many cases of "shell-shock" that ensued in the wake of the war. When it became clear these were not the result of any organic damage to the afflicted soldiers, he directed his attention to these cases as examples of traumatic neurosis. He hypothesized that the personality had been overwhelmed or that a breach had been made in its protective shield by horribly terrifying events. Such a breach would result either from the massive nature of the stimuli or because the personality had been caught by surprise, unable to hyperinvest its protective wall to resist the onslaught of events, or from a combination of both factors. Freud's thinking has been rediscovered—as the wheel so often is—in the aftermath of Vietnam as the now well-publicized "posttraumatic stress syndrome," and it is just such a syndrome we wish to prevent for a child by enabling him to protect himself by the preparation we give him in advance of the stresses to which he must be subjected. The quotes around the "new" in the title of this chapter refer to the basis of these thoughts in Freud's thinking of so long ago.

I shall try basically to bring up just three points about preparation, two of which evolve directly from Freud's thoughts. The principal goal of preparation is to help a child be ready for stressful events, for changes, or new events, so that he can activate or hyperinvest his protective mechanisms—preparation is protection. The second point is that the ultimate aim of preparation is not the avoidance of pain, anxiety, or distress, but rather to prevent the child from being overwhelmed or traumatized by events, to enable him to contain and ultimately master the event with the help of the protective preparation. The third point concerns the role of the mother in such preparation, so as to make it more effective.

CHILDREN TAKEN BY SURPRISE

I consult fortnightly with the pediatric house staff at one of our local hospitals. The residents can bring any cases or topics they wish to discuss and have often helpfully brought for discussion instances where they have been uncomfortable with what medical necessity has forced upon them. Recently they described the case of a little boy of three whose mother brought him to the Clinic because of two warts on the base of his penis. To treat these warts, it had been necessary to hold the little boy down, and the force that had been required, and the area they had to treat, had combined to provoke a terrified reaction in their little patient. This had distressed them, and they asked me what they should do in these situations; was there anything they could do in the future so that they would not have to terrify a three-year-old?

As we talked, it became clear the key here was preparation. Had the child been prepared? Could he have been prepared while in the Clinic? Should he have been sent home with his mother to get prepared and to have returned on another day? It turned out that the child had not been prepared for any treatment, as the mother had not known what, if any, treatment there might be. In the hustle and bustle of a typical, busy large hospital outpatient clinic, it had not seemed timely to tell the mother what was to transpire and to leave her alone with her son for some minutes to explain it to him. It turned out not to have been enough for the doctor to have explained to the boy as he sat on his mother's lap. It did not seem feasible to send the mother home, the child untreated, so that apparently she would have paid for nothing, for no care. She might even have taken offense at the inconvenience a return trip would have required and never come back. It did eventuate that the treatment involved would require multiple trips to the Clinic, so that the idea of sending her home at the initial visit would not have been as bad as we thought at first. This is not an unusual event in any pediatric outpatient setting. What may be unusual is the opportunity the house staff had to air their distress in a suitable forum.

What is needed here to help the young house officers in coping with their problems? First, I believe, would be all the support possible for their distress at the terror caused the little boy, for their wish to explore other possible ways of handling the situation. Second, I would guess, would be some ironclad, institutionalized clinic rule or policy, starting with the basic statement that no procedure is ever done on a child who is not prepared for it by the parent. If one starts here, then the exceptions become easier to identify: if the procedure is a medically urgent or emergency one, the child and parent would not be sent home for preparation; any exceptions to the policy would have to be cleared with the senior outpatient department pediatrician, or guidelines evolved with him. Only with rules of this nature could the house officers resist the pressures of administration, parents, and other staff to get along with it, get it done now—which simply means for the convenience of all the adults, convenience of all save the child. Third would be the availability of an outpatient department child life worker on call to help deal with the unavoidable emergencies, a person with special experience to whom the house staff could turn for assistance.

Incidentally, when the little boy returned to the Clinic, he manifested no fear of the doctors, to their great relief. I did not, unfortunately, have a good opportunity to discuss with them my distress at this outcome. I know that the experience of being overwhelmed, such as the boy endured, leaves its mark in the form of some sleep, eating, or other behavioral disturbance, and I was not happy his defenses were apparently operating to make the scene of his overwhelming so innocuous. That meant to me that the event and its psychological effects had become split apart from one another, making the event's ultimate mastery much less likely.

This brief vignette opens up many avenues for discussion and consideration. Is it really worthwhile to go to such lengths to prepare the child for such a relatively minor procedure? Why this emphasis on the mother, her explaining at home—a point to which I shall return. To approach the first question, I would like to go back to an episode from many years ago in which I was discussing the topic of preparation with the director of a daycare center. The question that arose then was what do you do if the horse has already gone from the barn, when you learn of a child's need for preparation only after the event, after the need has been bypassed? The example given was of a kindergarten boy who arrived late one morning in tears, his bloodied mouth only partially cleansed, minus four front teeth that had just been extracted. The baby teeth had apparently been blocking and endangering the normal eruption of the permanent teeth beneath them. The child had not been prepared for the extractions and, as the mother accompanying him said, "If I had known it was going to be that bad, I would never have let them do it." The procedure had been explained to her in the child's absence after the dentist's initial examination and evaluation. The only preparation the child got was the dentist's announcement to him, "Now I'm going to take out your four front teeth."

PREPARATION IS PROTECTION—PROTECTION IS A WAY OF LIFE

The daycare center director was asking me how we can ever prevent such horrors from happening. We agreed that all of them could never be eliminated, but perhaps there were some things that could be done to reduce their incidence for some families. What we began to work on were two slogans or guiding principles, preparation is protection; protection is a way of life.

This daycare center had always operated with a gradual separation policy at the start of school, had always introduced new children into the group one by one, letting the children already there know exactly who was joining them and when. This had been done as part of the separation or introduction phase of starting to join the group. This center had always informed the children of any changes in school routine in advance of their implementation, always told the children in advance of any changes in teacher or school personnel, as well as the reasons for the changes. Any new experience, such as a trip to the grocery store or fire station, had been carefully explained and discussed in advance. These things had been done out of respect for the children and as part of simply good educational management to facilitate the children's maximum use of the new experience or maximum adaptation to any change.

It was possible now, under the pressure of emphasizing preparation, to see that all these policies also fit under the rubric of preparation, and the decision was made of simply identifying the policies as preparation to stress the importance of preparation. What had previously been a bit of a silent policy now became most overt. This was not just for the benefit of the parents, but also for the benefit of the school personnel who had been implementing the policy of preparation without being fully aware of the significance of what they were doing. Preparation as protection and protection as a way of life were now discussed as an integral part of the school's gradual separation policy, and it became a topic for group meetings with the parents. The director explained at these meetings how seriously her center took its responsibility to keep the children safe and protected. She listed preparation as one aspect of parental functioning of protection assumed by the center. In this fashion, the center could communicate to the parents the importance of preparation as a way of life and not just something called into play in a very special or unusual circumstance. Only if parents are geared always to prepare their children in all possible situations can they call a halt to such traumatic experiences as the dental work described above.

WHAT IS PREPARATION?

This leads us next to what parents, teachers, and many others expect of preparation, and here we run into a couple of common misconceptions we should address. One of these is that our job is finished when we have told a child what to expect, whether it involves a hospitalization or a new child entering the class, or a substitute teacher coming on the scene for a few days. Informing about the reality can be described as not the end point, but rather as the means to an end point, which is finding out about a child's thoughts or fantasies about the upcoming event. In announcing a new teacher for the group and why she is coming, if one waits long enough and knows enough to listen for it, sooner or later a child will ask, "Will she know about our rules and how things work here?" What the child wants to know is whether or not he is going to be safe with the new teacher, kept in good control, and preparation will be successful when this fear of this has been brought out and addressed.

I remember from pediatric days helping a mother prepare a four-year-old for a brief hospitalization for relatively minor surgery, the removal of a small cyst from his buttock. I had an absolutely optimal situation in which to work, as the mother was not anxious about the procedure, and in our Air Force Hospital she had to be admitted with the child to do his nursing, as we had no pediatric nurses. The procedure went well and the little boy was discharged after but a few days' stay. The mother called me, however, quite soon to tell me she was faced with an unexpected sleep problem with her son. Although we had been careful not to refer to anesthesia as "being put to sleep," but rather as receiving a special medicine that would keep him from feeling any pain while it would seem as if he were asleep, the mother sensed he feared going to sleep lest he awake again with a hurt he had not had previously. This she had discussed with him, and all I could do was support what she was doing, adding the suggestion that she tell him about this as a goodnight story. She called me a few days later to report no success; all I could do was to tell her to just keep at it. Many days later I heard the end of the story when the mother saw me about a sibling. One night, when she was repeating the bedtime story for the umpteenth time, how the little boy was safe at home but still sometimes was afraid as if he were back at the hospital, even though he was safe at home, her son added the crucial detail in saying, "And the hospital can't come here, can it, Mommy?" I don't know why he had that fantasy. I can only guess about an age- and phase-appropriate projection of his aggression or newly forming conscience, but I do know all the preparation and hard work were to no avail until his fantasy had been elucidated and the obvious reassurance given and accepted.

I used to wonder why our preparation failed. I still would like to know for sure why this little boy had so much trouble postoperatively. Only slowly did I realize that our preparation had not failed, had, in fact, served well its role of allowing the boy to bring to his mother the fantasy that caused him so much distress. With his fantasy known and dealt with, his mother and I could feel that the surgery was finally mastered.

Another common misconception is that preparation should eliminate all pain, anxiety, and stress. In her excellent article on "Why Worry Helps," Lauter (1978) laments the idea that preparation for surgery or a hospitalization might be thought of as a way to eliminate fear because it is better for a child to feel reasonable fear of difficult experiences than to be encouraged to suppress all anxiety. She says that unless fear is aroused beforehand, the person will not be motivated to get ready for danger and will have a low tolerance for stress when the crisis is at hand. She writes of being realistic and not frightening the child. She well understands the importance of parents having their own anxieties under control, as well as the child having the opportunity to bring his fears and fantasies as the end point of preparation. I was impressed with her understanding of the protective function of anxiety whose absence Freud pointed to so many years ago as the crucial factor in whether or not a severe stress was going to be damaging to the personality.

All I would want to add is something we have learned from bitter experience in helping mothers prepare their children for the hospital, and that is that there are always surprises one cannot anticipate. The best way to cope with this is honestly to tell the child of it and to have him keep alert for any surprises he can then, after the fact, report to his parents. This works out rather well, actually, as it helps to create in the old-enough child an attitude of prepared, calm alertness, which is an optimal preparation for the constructive use of signal anxiety.

PROTECTION IS A PARENTAL FUNCTION

If preparation is viewed as protection against any harmful overwhelming, we are talking at base about a parental function, one that begins as a maternal function. With all the current national emphasis in all media about teaching children to "Say no!" about drugs, it would seem worthwhile to devote some thought to how a child acquires a proper sense of self-protection.

It starts with a mother's loving investment of her child, of his body in the very first months of life. By the care she gives her infant, a mother communicates that the infant is of value, that his body is of the greatest value. All that she does proclaims that he and his body are worthy of the greatest possible protection. In her work with those providing toddler daycare, E. Furman (this volume, Chapter 7; 1992; 1993) has emphasized the importance of the toddler's ability to protest pain, to seek help when hurting. How much this ability is related to the mother, she illustrates with the example of the 19-month-old with an acute otitis media. The caregiver had noticed that the child did not feel well, was a bit listless, and had called his mother to come to the daycare center. Only on her arrival did the child start to cry with the severe pain anyone would experience with bilateral bulging ear drums that are the hallmark of this illness.

Just as the loving investment of the child's body is a first-year function of the mother-child relationship, so the struggle to teach safety is the second-year task that keeps mothers of active toddlers both slim and exhausted. Her constant watchfulness and chasing of her toddler is just an essential feature of life with him, one that teaches him, despite his protest, the importance of safety. Slowly, over time, these maternal attitudes become the child's own. This is a process so well described in the, to us, well-known story of the three-year-old starting nursery school. Mother asked, at the end of a six-week gradual separation period, how the day had gone, had the child missed her? When the little girl said that she had, the mother asked what she had done, rather expecting the child would have gone to her teacher for support and sympathy. But the little girl replied, "When you weren't there to love me, I just loved myself a little bit more."

If we see protection of the child as a maternal function, something a mother teaches by providing it, something a child gradually takes unto himself from his mother, then a number of things become clear. It explains why, whenever possible, daycare homes or preschools send home notes to parents about coming events and changes in school routine, for instance when there is a change of teachers in the classroom, or when a child with an abnormality or deformity is being added to the group. It is right for us to let mother do the preparing whenever possible. This thinking explains why we think that the preparation of the child by the mother allows the child to take a bit of mother along with him when he has to undergo experiences such as a hospitalization or a medical procedure, even one as simple as getting an injection at a routine pediatric visit. This thinking also explains why it is best, even after preparation by the mother, to have her physically present for these experiences whenever possible.

Perhaps it is worth our while to take a close look at each one of these instances. One very nice aspect of the Lauter (1978) article referred to above is the author's clarity about the need for mother and father both to have their anxieties under control before explaining future events to their child so that the explanations do not inadvertently become means of allowing parents to transfer their anxiety to their child. This is something explicitly to be discussed with parents in advance of their preparing their child, both the importance of their doing the preparation as well as the importance of their being in control themselves about what they are preparing the child for. Early childhood professionals and daycare center directors do this when they send home notes asking the parents to check with them if they have any questions about the content of the notes sent home; physicians should do this when they discuss medical procedures in advance with the parents. This is an instance when the music and the lyrics have to be in synchrony, and we all know too well examples of when parents have used all the right words to explain something, such as a death in the wider school family, only to have done so in a fashion that could only terrify the listener.

I remember my chagrin when two mothers repeated back to me what we had discussed they would say to their child about the death of a mother of a classmate. One reported having started with, ''I have something very sad we have to talk over together.'' The other started with, ''I have something very scary to tell you.'' It is not hard to imagine how both these talks went, how one contained anxiety, and the other spread it. I remember also when a daycare center had a child who was so often out of control that his day had to be progressively limited until it reached the few hours that he could manage without losing control, frightening the other children, and disrupting the classroom. After he had well managed the shortened day for a period, it was time to increase his attendance in the classroom, and the children had to be prepared for this. The director reported that something went awry, and the more the teachers prepared the children, the more they seemed to get upset. Careful listening to the preparation soon explained to the director what was going on. In their anxiety about the child's increasing his hours, their worry if they could contain the child, the teachers were reviewing with the children all the horrors of the child's earlier behavior, only in passing, as it were, speaking to all his gains in control which should have been the focus of their discussion.

Lauter (1978) is very clear and direct about the need to offer parents consultation until their anxiety is under control, even suggesting referral to a mental health professional if it becomes clear that a parent's anxiety is too great to be mastered in further discussion at school, daycare center, or the doctor's office. If a mother cannot prepare her child, one can have someone substitute for her—a teacher, a doctor, a child life worker, a father. To prepare a child in this fashion has its limitations if a mother cannot follow up an explanation of reality facts.The greatest limitation is, however, in the situation involving a hospitalization or medical procedure when the mother's anxiety continues unabated. It is obviously best then, if possible, to have father substitute for the mother.

When a mother can be physically present with her anxiety well contained, then one approaches the optimal situation. Such a mother can well utilize the child life workers who function at most of our local pediatric inpatient services. All who deal with children should be aware of the services offered by child life workers and alert families to their availability (this volume, Chapter 12).

At one of our weekly Hanna Perkins School case conferences we recently discussed a kindergarten child now in excellent fettle. At nine months she had been hospitalized twice in short order, the second time for ten days, and it was a time of extensive, multiple and medically necessary procedures. There were two aspects of this little child's story that seemed important to me. Following the hospitalization, she had recurrent anxiety attacks and a severe sleep problem that literally took years to master. The story of the work with this very capable mother and of her work with her child was a pleasure to hear unfold as it ultimately led to complete mastery of the severe preverbal stress the medical necessities had engendered. Equally remarkable was all the mother had been able to do while the child was in the hospital to try to minimize the stresses to which she was exposed. Let me quote briefly from the clinical report: "Mother was with her throughout and tried to protect her from being overwhelmed, at times insisting that doctors stop procedures and allow her to hold and feed the child until she could reintegrate herself. She made sure no IV was put in the right hand so that the child could have the preferred thumb available for self-comfort." In hearing the story, it was very difficult not to feel that the mother's protection during the hospitalization made the traumatic experience subsequently masterable even though the trauma itself could not be avoided—a contribution of great significance.

In talking before about the significance of the mother's role in preparation and in protection, the third point I mentioned had to do with "taking a bit of mother along" to any experience by the preparation the mother does. This is, as mentioned before, a good way to help a child internalize his mother's role as protector. E. Furman quotes Anna Freud in telling of a four-year-old in the Hampstead Residential Nursery during World War II when the child was temporarily separated from his mother. He was overheard one morning saying to himself as he was dressing, "Now button up, darling, so you won't be cold." There was no doubt whose words he was repeating to himself.

Most specifically when a mother prepares a child and allows him his anxiety, but shows him how to contain it by her example and her explanation, she is facilitating her child's ability to use anxiety as an aid, to use signal anxiety, as opposed to letting anxiety be the master that overwhelms. Years ago, in writing a paper about developmental sequences in the verbalization of affects, I (1978) described a mother telling her son that if, in her absence, he was afraid, it was okay; he needed just to know he was afraid, know of what, stay in control, and they would discuss it when she returned. In this instance, she was teaching him about signal anxiety, how to contain it, and how ultimately to use it for mastery.

PREPARATION HELPS WITH RECOVERY FROM ILLNESS

Lauter (1978) quoted research done at the Massachusetts General Hospital on the role preoperative preparation played in cutting down the use of postoperative medication, in shortening postoperative hospital stays. I tried in vain to locate the paper in question and finally turned to a medical directory. I found one of the authors living now in Dallas. I wrote Dr. Egbert there and was able to initiate a delightful exchange of letters. He was pleased someone was still interested in such an old paper of his and in sending me the reprint I wanted, included a couple of his more recent papers. He is an anesthetist, obviously a wise and sensitive man. One of his papers was written to exhort anesthetists to talk with their patients preoperatively (Egbert, Battit, Turndorf, and Beecher, 1963). He acknowledges that this is difficult for many of his colleagues who go into anesthesiology in part because of their interest in chemistry and the machines of their trade, perhaps by choice not so interested in interpersonal relations. In suggesting preoperative talks with patients for anesthetists, he really starts at square one, advising his colleagues that they should start by introducing themselves.

To make his point, he tells a brief story about a friend of his who was in the hospital awaiting a cervical fusion, a neck operation, the following day. The surgeon entered the room, lifted up the patient's gown, palpitated her abdomen, and reassured her that the removal of her gall bladder would not take more than an hour. "Only then did they introduce each other and not in a very friendly fashion!"

I include this story for a number of reasons, the first being that I enjoyed it so much, I wanted to share it with others. It is, however, a good example of what we let happen to ourselves as patients once we are in the hospital. I know this was not the point of his story, but how strange that a grown woman would let a total stranger enter her room and examine her abdomen without a word of introduction or explanation. I think we all, in our anxiety, regress so that we too often become like helpless children once we are in the hospital, forgetting our most basic human rights. This is something that can happen to mothers when their children are in the hospital, something that child life workers can help them prevent, something that the mother reported at the Hanna Perkins conference did not let happen to her when she interceded so properly for her nine-month-old daughter. I include this story also to remind all of us that sometimes we can find people like Dr. Egbert when we need them, and that they are worth searching for.

Egbert's and his colleagues' (Egbert, Battit, Welch, and Bartlett, 1964) paper on preparation of patients for surgery concerned 97 adults who had abdominal surgery, about half of whom had careful preparation, the others did not. Postoperative narcotics were reduced by half in the prepared group whose hospital stays were reduced by 2.7 days compared with the control group. Repeatedly, we have the experience with children at Hanna Perkins whose parents we have helped prepare their children and about whom the surgeons remark on how well the children physically tolerated the procedure. I would love to interest child life workers, pediatric surgeons, pediatricians, or even insurance carriers and governmental health authorities in doing a study about preparation of children for surgery, preparation through the parents assisted by the child life workers as compared to families that do not receive such assistance. It is very hard for me to believe that such a study would not prove that the saved hospital days would amply compensate for the salaries of a team of child life workers. It would be nice to have the insurance carriers pushing for all hospitals to have a staff of child life workers to help parents and children prepare for surgery and other medical experiences!

PREPARATION ENHANCES ENJOYMENT

I want to close by bringing an example of the positives of preparation in contrast to always thinking of preparation as a kind of double negative, only preventing bad things happening. I like this last example also as it demonstrates how preparation can lead to integration, and hence the rich enjoyment of new experiences as well as the mastery of difficult ones. I eat lunch on Thursdays in our Hanna Perkins Kindergarten, and one of my table mates there is a little boy of whom I am quite fond, but a fellow who is a bit of a cynic, one who unfortunately can delight in putting others down when they are enjoying something. To my surprise and great pleasure at our last lunch, he was bubbling with joy and enthusiastically wanted to tell me of their year-end treat, a trip to the ice cream store. He showed me the map of their walk that his teacher had prepared for them in advance, showing all the buildings they would see on their walk, even the different texture of the walks themselves. "There were cobblestones right here," I was told as he pointed to the map. Then he showed me the chart of which flavors each had had, which were the favorite flavors. Finally, I saw the book his teacher had prepared about the trip, describing all they had done.

It was a simple trip, a simple common life experience, but by loving preparation it had been turned into the event of the year, richly enjoyed by all. I think it a good story with which to end.

To summarize briefly the few points I have wanted to make: first, I do believe that preparation is protection, protection not from distress or discomfort, but from being overwhelmed. Second, preparation and protection in this sense should be a way of life, a basic of child rearing and education that starts almost when life starts. Teaching children to say "no" to drugs in adolescence is laudable, but unless a child has grown up taught to value himself and protect himself from the start, such teaching will have limited success. Third, I have tried to emphasize the mother's role in protecting her child, our need to support her in transmitting protection to her child, supporting her really being there whenever possible.

4

Helping Children Cope
with Stress

ROBERT A. FURMAN, M.D.

In this chapter, I shall develop three points. First, stresses are not to be avoided when they or their derivatives impinge on the classroom; in fact, they may offer optimal opportunities for effective preschool education. Second, in dealing with stresses it is impossible to avoid dealing with feelings. This seems a proper area for the attention of the preschool educator. Third, dealing effectively with stresses as well as with feelings requires a cooperative relationship with parents of the preschooler, particularly with the primary mothering person; I shall bring in some ideas on how to establish and maintain such a relationship.

What do I mean by a stress? It could be said that anything that imposes an extra demand on a child's ability to cope, often something that is new and different, is a stress. But as examples are so much more meaningful than definitions, let me share a recent experience.

A STRESS ARISING IN SCHOOL

I was eating lunch in our Hanna Perkins Nursery School with three five-year-old boys and an almost four-year-old girl. Lunch was suddenly interrupted by the appearance at the door of two policemen with a little boy who appeared to be four or five. This caused quite a stir. The head teacher managed the intrusion by finding out that the police had found the boy wandering about the street near the school and had assumed he was one of ours. After being told he was not and accepting some suggestions about how to approach him to find out his name, where he lived, and where his mother might be, they left.

You can imagine the melody that lingered after their departure. There were many different ways the teacher at my lunch table could have managed this. She could have hushed the children and urged them back to their meal, ignoring the interruption and the rather scary implication of the lost child. But she said, "My, that was some surprise, wasn't it?" Then she turned to the most concerned-looking little boy and asked, "What did you think about that, Jim?" "It scared me," he replied. When asked why, he continued, "Had that boy been bad? Is that why the cops had him?" The teacher explained the reality, that he had been lost and that the police were trying to help him. "Will they hurt him?" was the next question, and the teacher repeated they were trying to help him. After a bit of silence, one of the boys asked, "Where was his mother?" Before the teacher could answer, the third boy said, "My mother told me if I was ever lost I should go and find a policeman to help me." Picking up on this, the teacher asked what he might say to the policeman. A lively discussion ensued with many good suggestions. Everyone practiced telling his name. All agreed one boy was well prepared who had learned his address and telephone number. When lunch was finishing, all were busy thinking about and practicing learning their addresses, even the under-four-year-old girl.

A stress was imposed on the class by the appearance of the police and the lost boy. Instead of ignoring it, the teacher got the children to say what they felt about it, what they thought about it, before reviewing the reality with them. Then she allowed the children to make a good educational experience out of the episode. I might add that when I visited for lunch the next week, the little girl greeted me by telling me her home address. She let me know, among other things, what she had learned from the event of the previous week.

I know that many teachers could give such examples. Although the specifics are unique, the interruptions caused by such happenings are not. Let us look for a moment at what might have gone through the teacher's mind. I am sure she realized that if she did not deal with the event directly, there was going to be a rough lunch ahead and difficulty with afternoon activities because of the children's upset or anxiety about the episode. So she immediately brought it up for discussion by saying quite mildly what she felt—surprised. After she had shared her feeling, Jim, who looked petrified, could follow suit. The feelings of the moment spoken to, the teacher then clarified the reality so that each one knew just what had happened.

If we look at every stress in the way this one was looked at, there will usually be a learning situation to be found because stresses are an unfortunate but unavoidable part of life. And this is the first point I want to make: stresses are best managed by not avoiding them because (1) they offer important opportunities for learning experiences; (2) their management can remove the interferences they would otherwise impose on the school situation.

A STRESS BROUGHT TO SCHOOL

I would like now to bring up another example, one in which the stress was not so readily clear because it arose outside of school. Cal was between three and a half and four years old when the episode occurred. Although still a bit hyperactive and rambunctious, he had finally settled well into preschool after a bit of a difficult separation from his mother. One day his teacher noted a definite increase in his hyperactivity, returning to the level it had occupied during his first few weeks in school. She did not pay it too much attention until she saw him attacking one of the other but larger boys. The other boy had been caught off guard and, although not really hurt, was crying as if he had been. Rather than showing remorse or distress, Cal just seemed excited by what he had done.

Knowing Cal quite well by this time, as she removed him, the teacher asked what had upset him so this morning. Cal replied, ''Well, he's all broken up now.'' ''What's that all about?'' the teacher asked, but got no answer. Shortly after Cal had seemed to settle again, trouble started in the block corner where he demolished another's project. The teacher was quite firm in removing him the second time and Cal said, ''Pow, I knocked it all down.'' As the teacher started to tell Cal firmly that this had to get under control, he said, ''Well, that's what they did to that old house. Pow, and it was all gone!''

This was the further clue the teacher had needed to elicit from Cal the story that, on the way to school, the car had stopped for a light at a corner where a wrecking crew was just finishing the demolition of a building that had required but 24 hours for its disappearance. She spoke at once to how scary it was to see a home disappear just overnight and practically right in front of his eyes. There was no verbal agreement from Cal, but he relaxed and got himself in control.

The teacher asked Cal whether he would be willing to tell the other children about it at group time because, although it had been a bit scary, it was something unusual and interesting the other children might like to know about. She assisted and censored his presentation a bit, using the discussion also to explain the upsets of the morning to the others who had been frightened and puzzled by Cal's outbursts. In addition, she knew well that a number of Cal's classmates had seen the same sight as he had on their way to school, and she reasoned if it had upset Cal that much, maybe it had bothered some of the others a bit also. She reviewed with them all how hard it was to see something destroyed so suddenly, that this would not happen to their homes, that the crane operators worked very skillfully and carefully, and that the house was torn down to prepare the lot for some new construction. They all guessed what that might be and then watched through the spring with great interest, often bringing daily reports of the construction of a small office building on the site.

Here again the stress was approached and not avoided, the feelings dealt with first, the reality then explained in a constructive learning situation. What is different is that the source of the stress was not known to the teacher and was detected only as a consequence of her dealing with the change in Cal's behavior. Teachers often use changes in the behavior patterns of children as an indication that they may have experienced a stress.

There is an observation that seems important to interject here. Some people have an excellent inherent capacity for evidencing all outward appearance of calm while being upset inside, and can immediately discuss upsetting events without communicating their upset. The teacher who managed the police and lost

boy episode did just that. Later in the week, when I compli-
mented her on her management, her response to me was, "Gosh,
that scared me! I didn't know what had happened!" But she did
not pass her distress on to the children, did not tell them what
she told me. Rather, she had used the more neutral word "surprised," thus sharing her distress matter-of-factly, without
spreading it to the children and increasing what they were feeling.
In explaining stresses to children it is not easy to tread the fine
line between telling them enough and frightening them with too
much fact or feeling. I know little to say as a guideline, except
to point out the possible danger, underline the importance of our
protective as well as educational role with the child, warn against
passing on our anxiety, and simply acknowledge it is not an
easy task.

Prevention of stresses or containment of anticipated stresses
through preparation whenever possible is a vital, related topic,
but one too large to approach here. What can be done is to
acknowledge the fact and include a helpful reference (see this
volume, Chapter 3).

THE ROLE OF FEELINGS

The episodes I have described went well for many reasons, fore-
most among them being the attention to the children's feelings
which prepared the way for the constructive explanations of the
stresses. By contrast, I would now like to describe two other
stressful situations that were not so approached and had quite
different outcomes, educationally and emotionally.

A few years ago I was working with the mother of a little
boy who came to the Hanna Perkins Kindergarten when his nursery school teacher of the prior two years expressed doubts to the
parents about the boy's ability to cope with the learning demands
that would be placed upon him in public school. Although the
problem was not quite as simple as I shall present it, our work
did hinge on a crucial incident. As he started school, it became
obvious to all that the basic reason why he could not learn related
to his inability to tolerate separation from his mother. When she
left, and in proportion as her day away from him increased, he
was unable to focus on his work. His attention, feelings, and

thinking apparently stayed with his mother, leaving when she did. As the mother and I together explored this difficulty, she could date its onset quite clearly to his first year in nursery school. Shortly after he began school at a bit over three, she was hospitalized for elective surgery for a ten-day period. She had delayed her surgery until he had started school, feeling that the school day would make the separation from her easier. She did not tell the school of her hospitalization; his transportation was managed by two other mothers with whom she had formed a car pool. Both she and the father felt that the nature of the surgery could not be explained to him, so they simply told him mother was going to the hospital for a few days. Both parents were anxious about the surgery and depressed by it, and could remember little of his reaction to his mother's absence. No further discussion or explanation was given to the boy.

The validity of the mother's retrospective understanding of her son's trouble was borne out by our work which basically consisted of her going back over this episode with him, discussing it as the origin of his trouble with mother leaving him. He was able to recapture his feelings of the time—sadness, worry, confusion. As he was able to do this and become informed about what had happened, in exact proportion could he allow her to leave and still be able to learn and function as an appropriate kindergartener. It became clear to both of us that he had felt if he was not allowed to know anything about such an important event as the disappearance of the mother, what right had he to learn about other things, the facts his teachers wanted to help him learn. There was also a bit of revenge in his attitude, "Since you would not teach me about that crucial episode, I will not learn anything in school. And when you get upset about that, it will serve you right." The unapproached stress that lay dormant for two years had grossly interfered with the boy's educability, until it was mastered.

Similar, but not identical, is the story of a little boy I saw some years ago in an evaluation. He was emotionally quite ill and his parents had for some time worried he was retarded. He was not quite four when I saw him, a terrified little boy, almost drowned in a heart-rending mixture of sadness and fear, etched all over his face. His mother, in her anxiety, had carefully taught him his colors and his numbers up to ten which he repeated on her command without expression, and yet also used appropriately when he was with me. In his session with me I asked him after a bit how he felt about seeing me, how he managed so bravely to leave his mother to be with me, a total stranger. He was at a complete loss to respond to my question, his face a blank. I told him I knew other boys had felt a bit sad or worried on leaving Mommy to be with me alone, but he continued to look blank. When I saw his parents later to discuss my impressions, they began by telling me how distressed he had been before and after his visit with me, with a marked increase in his frantic hyperactivity, a symptom I knew expressed his anxiety. As I talked with them about this, I found that the words sad, worried, scared were not known to the boy, had never been used or explained to him. No words about any feelings had been used with him, although they had been quite active educationally with teaching him his colors and numbers. With no words for feelings the boy had no means for coping with feelings except in the wild hyperactivity whose increase told us all about the stress he endured in seeing me.

As stresses should not be avoided but should be viewed as an appropriate task for the teacher to address and help with, so should feelings. The identification and verbalization of feelings can be taught or reinforced in school or center as the very proper province of the preschool educator. When we say that assisting a child to cope with stress is an educational task, we are talking about teaching a child how to deal with the realities that impinge upon him from the outside world. When we teach a child how to deal with his feelings, we are describing an educational approach to the realities that impinge upon him from within. It would seem to me that if a teacher cannot be of help in these vital areas of reality, a child is going to have a hard time understanding the reality, or perhaps the relevance, of the teacher's role. I cannot see how one can preserve a child's curiosity and love of learning unless one is willing and eager to teach him about those realities, inside and outside of him, that arouse his curiosity and about which he most wants to learn.

Actually, most teachers educate about feelings already, perhaps without giving it much thought. How many times a day we hear in the nursery school, ''No, Johnny, we do not hit when we are angry in school. We tell the other we don't like what they are doing, and we tell them to stop,'' or, ''Running and loud voices are for outside time, not for inside time.'' In these instances the teacher is directing herself to the mastery, containment, and control of feelings in the service of successful performance of certain school tasks.

If attention is paid to educating about feelings, what can a teacher do? It really starts with recognition and identification of feelings. Although most children come to school with an effective knowledge or awareness of what they are feeling, a surprising number may not know the words to go with what they are experiencing. When you simply say to a child, ''My, you look cross just now,'' or, ''It is hard for everyone the first few days at school, when it seems strange and scary,'' and when these statements are made as he experiences the feeling you are describing, you are identifying it for him.

I would love to see as a part of every early childhood teacher's report or evaluation a section covering the child's ability to identify appropriately his basic feelings of sadness, anger, fear, excitement, happiness. Next could come the more shaded subtleties of feelings, such as lonely as well as sad, cross or annoyed as well as angry, worried as well as scared, keyed up as well as excited, loving as well as happy. With these, too, many preschoolers may require some simple educational assistance. But I would like the evaluation to include some further observations. Can the child not only identify the basic feelings and their more subtle variations as he experiences them, but can he also effectively and properly put them into words? This is so often the first step toward the mastery and control of feelings (R. A. Furman, 1978).

PUTTING FEELINGS INTO WORDS

When what you feel can be put into a familiar word and you understand your state of mind, then you are better able to deal with it, in part because of prior experiences with the same feeling. When what you feel can be put into words, you are also able to begin to think about what to do to alleviate the feeling: seek help or understanding if you are scared, obtain comfort and sympathy when you are sad, seek redress or rectification when you are angry, share your feeling when you are happy. I mention these obvious facts to underscore just one aspect of putting feelings into words, i.e., after the initial or trial experiences, putting feelings into words is not an end in itself but the first step toward active mastery. This helps us to distinguish the improper use of verbalizing feelings that comes, for example, when some children use angry words to hit with. Proper would be saying, "I'm angry at you. I do not like what you are doing. It makes me very cross" as this communicates well what is wanted next: "I want you to stop that!" Improper would be saying, as I heard a boy just last week, "You're a stinky poo" which does little more than just hit the other with messy language. It will represent a transitional progressive step for the child who had only hit or thrown things or made a mess before, but it will not represent the achievement of what we mean by verbalizing feelings.

ROLE OF THE RELATIONSHIP WITH THE PARENTS

I would like to go back to Cal now, Cal of the demolished house. We do not know whether he tried to tell his mother on his drive to school that the crane had scared him and how she responded, or whether he had acted as if he had not seen the crane and she was therefore unaware of his fear. (Cal did not attend our school where such followup would have been possible, but was reported to me in a consultation.) How helpful it would have been to Cal and to his teacher if his mother could have reported to her that Cal had been frightened by the crane! Similarly, in the example of the mother who had been hospitalized just after her son had entered nursery school, how helpful it would have been to him and to his teachers if she had shared this with them!

I started with examples of stress in which the cooperative work of the parents was not essential, where the teachers were able on their own to understand and deal with the stresses, the episodes of the police and the lost boy and of Cal and his encounter with the crane.

But to be truly effective in dealing with stresses requires a working relationship with the parents, part of which is a free flow of information and observation, in both directions, between parents and teachers. This is true for the work with feelings as well. My first painful experience in preschool consultation concerned a very aggressive little boy in a daycare center. He was so aggressively out of control, there was question if they could keep him. I helped them to help the boy get in control by learning to put his anger into words. Just when our joint hard work had improved his behavior so much that exclusion was no longer considered, he suddenly stopped coming to the center. Contact with his mother explained what had happened. When angry at home, he had told his mother so and said she was a bad mother, all in response to a minor frustration. She told the teacher she was not about to have any child of hers talk to her that way and had "strapped him but good." When he said they had taught him this at day care, that ended day care. It taught us all the sad and painful lesson that work with feelings requires contact and work with parents as well. With hindsight it was clear that before starting work with the boy, his mother should have been told of the danger of exclusion because of his behavior. Then she might have been enlisted to assist the work of the Center, at least to be able to maintain his attendance. It might not have succeeded, could not be done after the fact, but would have been the proper approach.

How does one communicate with parents? How does one establish the type of relationship where the teacher can feel free to tell the parents of changes in behavior that puzzle her, and the parents can feel free and interested in sharing with the school changes in behavior or stresses that occur at home? If such a relationship had existed between school and the mother of the little kindergarten boy mentioned earlier, the chances are he could have been aided to deal with the stress of his mother's hospitalization at the time it occurred, without having to come to Hanna Perkins to work this through laboriously years later. How do you guide and help parents to discuss with you what is important for the school to know, without becoming involved in areas that are not properly your province?

I would like now to consider the task of establishing a working relationship with parents because it is an essential part of helping children cope with stress. If you feel you want to establish such working relationships with the mothering persons of your preschoolers for the purpose of being able more effectively to fulfill your role as a teacher, then you have already accomplished the largest part of the job, for such an attitude will be directly and indirectly conveyed to each mother from the time of your first contact. Such an attitude defines your role as being her helper in the unfolding development of her child, rather than as the judge of the mother's previous efforts at raising him. Such an attitude demarcates that you will be interested in what happens in the child's life and development at home, not out of wanton curiosity, but out of a desire to be of help to the child.

It is a great help to delineate the type of relationship you want to build with the mother at the time of her first inquiry about your school or center. During this initial contact one can begin to explain that the preschool years are marked by such important developmental changes that home and school must stay in close touch. Then you can give examples of how reactions to stresses at school may not show at school but rather at home in changes in behavior patterns, and how important it would be for you to know about them so that school demands can be geared appropriately to the child's level. Likewise, you can give examples of how stresses at home can alter a child's behavior at school, can interfere with his progress, unless they are known to you. You can point out how regular informal sharing of the changes in the child's development, behavior, and life circumstances can enable you to work together to help him become master of himself and what goes on about him. At some later point, perhaps in an introductory parent meeting, I would also give some examples of the types of situations you would like to know about, situations in which you could be of help to the child—illnesses, deaths of pets or relatives, visits to the doctor, vacation plans, and so forth.

In approaching mothers in this fashion I have noted that some teachers, just like most mothers, underestimate the importance of their role. To the average mother the teacher is quite an awesome figure. You may be the first one to whom she has ever turned over the care of her child. You are different from relatives and sitters because the mother knows there are standards in school which her child must meet and which you will observe. Most mothers feel that you will be the first objective evaluator of all she has done, good and bad, in her child's first years. But that is not all. She will be building up this overestimation of you at a time when she is under the stress of separating from her child, realizing that a very special phase of her mothering of that child is coming to an end. And of course you realize who is the agent of this change—you!

If a teacher can accept that this is the way mothers view her, realistic or not, she can do much to ease a mother's discomfort. Just to focus on what lies ahead for the child implies complete acceptance of all that has transpired. To delineate for a mother the vital role you foresee for her in the preschool experience is also to imply that her work is not over, that she is still needed. If you can back up these attitudes with an understanding of her sadness and loss at separating from her child, of the change in her relationship to her child that school seems to demarcate, you will go a long way toward establishing the type of relationship we are talking about. Your understanding of a mother's feelings will help you know how much it means to her to be asked to participate in the child's separation from her at the start of school and to have your sympathetic and experienced guidance and support with it. In doing so you will begin to define the role you wish to fulfill in action—that of one who wants to work with a mother in furthering the full growth of her child.

In discussing these points with experienced teachers, I have often been told that at first many mothers want no part of such a relationship, want no part in participating during the separation days at the start of school. Unfortunately, there are a few such mothers. If we try to reach them and fail, "Nothing ventured, nothing gained." But in addition to the majority who will welcome such a participating role, I am aware of a not inconsiderable group who will ward off their sadness at separation from their child by a defensive turnaround in which they will exhibit to you a callous or light-hearted attitude to these stresses. Many of these mothers will not reveal to you the worthlessness they feel when their child starts school, but will defensively belittle the whole experience as of little importance. Some will even turn their worry about how you will judge them into an overly critical evaluation of you and your school. With a mother who defends her feelings in these ways, your mere acknowledgment of what you know many mothers feel at this time, along with your work with her, will often melt away the defenses. With some, a steady unruffled persistence in stressing the importance of the mother to her child and his schooling will slowly erode their attitude and bring about the kind of relationship we are seeking.

Incidentally, the rewards you will receive for such work with mothers will not come in superficial flattery or praise. Nobody really responds in this way to someone who has helped or understood them through a hard time. Rather, your reward will come in a silent respect that will show only in the cooperation you will enjoy. I recall wondering during my pediatric days whether the mothers really cared about the time I spent with them on sleeping, weaning, and toileting problems. Nobody ever praised me for this work the way parents often did when penicillin had miraculously turned a sick child into a well one. But when I left practice, I was stunned by the warm letters of deep appreciation I received for just those efforts I had thought had gone almost unnoticed.

Actually, teachers have most often asked me not how to start the type of working relationship we are discussing, but rather how to limit it once it has been established. How do you deal with the mother who reacts as though she has at last found a willing ear for all her troubles and wants to deluge you with them, especially marital ones. Some teachers stay at arm's length from mothers just for fear that they would not be able to cope with such situations. The mother who wants to use you to involve you with such difficulties wants to use you to help herself, not her child. But this would be a misuse of the working relationship we have been describing, since your role is to help the child and therefore being available and interested in all that impinges on him. So if a mother wants to tell you about marital discord, you can initially be just sympathetic, but, at the first opportunity, ask how she and her husband have dealt with the effects of this discord on the child because that is the only place where you can truly be of help. If this does not suffice to reestablish the nature of your role, you can ask whether the father had wanted her to discuss this with you (R. A. Furman, 1986). If that does not help, you can clearly delineate your role for this situation—to help both parents deal with the effects of the marital discord on the child, and to refer them to an appropriate agency, marriage counselor, or psychiatrist if they wish help for themselves. But if, in the case of marital discord, the parents together seek your help about the child, you could accomplish a great deal. You could help them to work together as parents in this area, such as how to explain that mothers and fathers sometimes have troubles and get to arguing with each other. You can urge them to keep their disputes private and to explain to the child that their disagreements are not his fault. I am not trying to be exhaustive on this issue, but merely trying to illustrate how the working relationship may operate, even in situations that threaten to pervert your role as helper to the child. I know I touch on an important topic only most superficially. My goal is to convey something of the feel for the nature of the working relationship with a mother and how it can be established and maintained.

5

Working with Parents

RUTH HALL

Establishing cooperative, mutually respectful relationships with parents is one of the most important tasks of preschool teachers and caregivers. It is a crucial part of their commitment to offer children the best care possible. We know that a child cannot do well under circumstances in which his parents and caregivers are unhappy with or distrustful of each other. Yet, in practice, opportunities to build such cooperative relationships are often hard to come by and/or neglected. Poor communication between caregivers and parents can then easily lead to adversarial positions, especially if the child manifests a difficulty. For example, when a child is dropped off in the early morning to the care of teacher A, transferred an hour or so later to teacher B whose job it is to provide a sound preschool curriculum to the children in her care for five to seven hours, then passed on to teacher C until pickup time, there is little chance for useful communication to take place between the parent and teachers. The teacher whose task it is to educate the child rarely sees the parent at all. Such an unfortunate impasse can, likewise, develop in a half-day preschool when the child arrives and leaves by bus or by car pool. Under such circumstances, misunderstandings, competitive feelings, and placing of blame for misbehavior on the part of the child flourish. The parent and teachers each want the best care possible for the child and tend toward mistrust of the unknown caretaking partners. In whatever setting, the result is always unhappy and frustrating for the adults as well as detrimental for the child.

65

This chapter explores ideas on how to mitigate and present the development of adversarial attitudes between parents and caregivers, so that they can successfully share in the joint task of helping each child to grow. I shall present vignettes from real situations and out of these try to identify the principles used to guide interactions in working with parents. The case examples come from my work as on-site consultant to a number of daycare centers, a community service provided by our Cleveland Center for Research in Child Development. As a consultant I have the opportunity to build relationships with the staff through regular meetings with the director and teachers, and I get to know the setting through weekly observation visits in the classrooms. The parents know about my participating role and may ask to consult with me or accept the director's suggestion to do so.

THE CASE OF MARTIN AND HIS PARENTS

I was asked to meet with Martin's parents because they were concerned about his reluctance to go to his center each day. The parents implied they suspected a certain teacher was not kind to him or that there was a "personality clash" as had happened with their older daughter at another school. The teachers had described the almost three-year-old boy as pleasant, cooperative, interacting well with peers, and fitting well into the classroom routine. The boy had been attending for only two months; this was his first experience in care away from home. I explored with the parents how their son had reacted to entering school and what his care had been like prior to that. They described a vigorous child who was very different from their compliant older daughter. The girl had been in daycare settings from birth on and had accepted all changes with no upheaval. Since this was not the child about whom I was being consulted, I set aside my sense of alarm at hearing this and concentrated on the information given about the boy. Though Martin seemed to enjoy himself once at school, each morning he would dawdle, cling, cry, and say he wanted to stay home. This would go on for an hour or more as the family prepared for the day. The parents mistook his preference for being with them for a sign that all was not right at school. Prior to entrance to daycare he had been cared for predominantly by his mother, with some afternoons spent at a well-known neighbor's home with her children. The parents were puzzled also because their son, normally a sound sleeper, was waking each night in great distress. These classic symptoms of separation pain fit well with the history of recent changes in care arrangements. The parents went on to allude to their concern about the possible personality clash with one of the teachers. They were quick to assure me that they were pleased with the overall program and felt confident their child was receiving proper care, attention, and education.

They gave the following example of the reason for their worry. Martin reported one day that the teacher had told him he could not have a birthday cake at school. They were clearly angry and said they had seen a birthday celebration on their visit to the school prior to enrolling their child. They could at last share their idea that perhaps their son resisted coming to school each day out of anxiety about being with this teacher. They asked if I had been in the classroom to visit their child and observe his interactions with the teacher in question. I could say that I had been and was very puzzled and saddened to hear of their concern, as I knew the teacher to be conscientious and loving in her care of children. I could also tell them of my impression of their son as being an essentially normal, capable, feelingful little fellow. He had interacted comfortably with peers and *all* teachers and had not seemed distressed. He was able to make his needs known and was working hard at accomplishing self-care tasks, which is the job for all toddlers. I could understand their feelings about the birthday situation but could only believe there must be some simple explanation. It made no sense to me either, for I too had observed many birthday celebrations at the school. I hoped they would not delay in telephoning the teacher to learn what situation could have led their boy to believe such a disappointing thing, especially since his birthday was coming in only two weeks. Martin was clearly trying to tell them an important feeling from school, but the translation had to be faulty and could only be remedied by a talk with the teacher. I was sure she would set things right. With the parents' permission, I talked with the teachers too and learned the boy had asked to share in a birthday cake for a teacher from another class held in another room during nap time. I speculate he was trying to tell mother of his disappointment and his message was misconstrued, falling as it did on the parents' uneasy suspicions.

I spoke to the parents about how important it is for their child to feel that Mommy knows what happens at school. Frequent, detailed exchange of daily happenings, good and bad, between mother and teacher help the child feel that even though Mommy is not present, her wishes and ideas are known to his teachers and guide his care while he is with them. He can feel less "on his own" then, and therefore more receptive and capable. The parents were pleased to think of school in this way, but had thought they should not bother the teacher too much, fearing anger about this might then fall on their child. I stressed that a teacher's job is made harder when she knows nothing of a child's home life.

We could then take up the feelings a toddler has about changes in care. I described the ways a child tells feeling messages through behaviors, such as their boy was doing with his morning distress and sleep disturbance. These were messages about his missing his mother while at school. He seems to find school pleasant enough; it is just that his most important anchor in life was not there—Mommy. It takes time to adjust to such changes. I suggested they talk with their boy about these feelings and again recommended frequent talks with the teacher to let her know how lonely Martin was feeling. The teacher could then share those times at school with the boy and offer to call the mother so they could touch base. I encouraged the mother to arrange daily telephone talk time with both her son and his teacher for a while in order to facilitate mutual sharing about feelings and events. Such calls need not take long, but they go far in helping a child replenish "Mommy loves me" feelings, as well as promoting and building a comfortable, trusting relationship between teacher and parent. This "ounce of prevention" can keep little problems and misunderstandings from growing into big ones. Telephone calls are especially useful in daycare situations where shift changes often result in a child being dropped off to one teacher and picked up from another.

LISTENING TO THE PARENTS

What can be learned from this vignette? The most obvious idea of course is the need for open lines of communication that are used frequently, between teacher and parent. If this parent had shared her feelings and the boy's morning distress with the teacher, she would have been met with understanding and helpful suggestions about settling the child into the classroom with less pain. Knowing the teacher would have helped mother know that her child's statement, though honest and sincere, was incomplete, and clarification was but a telephone call away.

The reason I chose to focus most on this need for communication was in hopes of promoting the growth of a more trusting relationship between parent and teacher. This can come about only from shared experiences in which each is made aware of the other's commitment to the child whose care they share. This was my first meeting with these parents; I had no relationship with them either. I needed to proceed slowly, keeping in mind their already defensive stance. I could offer no opinions or advice until I knew more about them, their child, and their concerns. Therefore I began by listening to them tell of these things, trying to get the feeling of "standing in their shoes." Experience has taught me that there is no substitute for this phenomenon in establishing genuine communication. Once a parent feels that you have truly listened to his or her feelings and ideas and have displayed understanding and respect for them, then he or she will be more open to hearing your ideas. This is only the first step in building a relationship, and must be repeated many times if you wish to have ongoing influence on the way a parent deals with his or her child. I have come to know that no matter how incomprehensible an attitude or behavior may seem when first noted, it can be understood if enough of the right details that have led up to it can be learned. The vignette described offers an example of this.

The following is a more subtle example of understanding through listening. A mother complained that for the past three to four weeks her daughter had become blatantly provocative and simultaneously fearful of injury, yet ran away in terror if anyone tried to comfort her or inspect minor bumps or bruises. The mother reported an accident in the home in which a visiting child had broken her arm. The child's mother had been angry, accusing this child's mother of poor supervision. In talking of this accident to the child, I said it had been no one's fault. The child vigorously contradicted me, saying, "It was my mommy's fault, she said so!" The mother then recalled saying, in sarcasm,

"Oh, of course, I put that chair right there so J. would fall on it." This poor little one was trying to make sense of a mommy she loved and trusted who might at any moment decide to cause her to break her arm. Her provocations were terrified attempts to take charge of the situation and get it over with. Her fear of allowing anyone to inspect an injury had to do with her idea that the friend's arm had fallen off entirely and was sewn back on. She wanted to learn for herself if a body part was falling off or not.

ASSESSING PARENTAL FUNCTIONING

Let us return now to another aspect of the first interview described. One of the things I was trying to evaluate was what sort of parents were these? It is imperative if one wishes to offer counsel about parenting to anyone, to have some idea of that person's concept of being a parent. E. Furman (1969b) has described parenthood as a developmental phase. She outlines this phase as one of great emotional flux and flexibility, during which new ideas and models of identification combine with old ones to form a realistic functioning equilibrium in the self as parent. An especially helpful guideline in assessing a person's progress into this phase is the degree to which the parent feels responsible for the well-being of the child. For the healthy parent, the child's joy is the parent's joy, the child's pain, the parent's pain. If the child is injured or fails to develop as expected, the healthy parent feels guilt over this and urgently seeks to remedy the situation. When this requires great sacrifice on the part of the parent, it is given as a matter of course. This latter capacity, to tolerate pain for the sake of the child, is what enables a parent to permit a teacher or therapist, once a relationship has been established, to discuss very painful truths about their child for the purpose of making things better. If the attributes just described are missing or inadequately developed, the prognosis for influencing the parent is guarded at best. What about this set of parents? Their reason for requesting the consultation, their child's pain, tells us they care very much about his distress and indicates them as being fully into the phase of parenthood. Both parents came, which indicated to me they work as a team and support one another. On the other hand, they seemed to have no idea of the child's feelings about being separated from mother for essentially the first time, which led me to feel they were quite out of tune and naïve about child development. Whether this could change, only further work could reveal.

THE CASE OF BOBBY AND HIS PARENTS

Let us turn now to a more complicated example of work with a set of parents over a two-year period. I chose this particular case because I thought it illustrated well the process of helping a mother get in tune with her child. This is an example of a classroom situation with which many teachers may be confronted. Its very dramatic nature makes the issues I wish to emphasize clearly visible and therefore useful for our purposes. For reasons of confidentiality, I shall present only the portions of the work that portray the working process.

I was first consulted about Bobby when he was almost three years old. He was being prepared to move from the toddler classroom at his daycare to a classroom for three- and four-year-olds. His teachers were concerned because of his frequent rages and unpredictable attacks upon other children. He was competent regarding self-care in eating, dressing, and toileting, but social skills were not progressing as they ought. He could not be trusted in the classroom without a teacher's very close supervision. His scowling countenance, inability to share toys, materials, or teacher's attention made other children wary of him and teachers impatient and resentful.

The staff knew little about his history except that he had been cared for at a nearby home daycare for infants prior to attending his present program. He had been in his current classroom for about one and a half years. His mother was thought to be devoted but hard-pressed by a job that required she be out of town several times each year for a week or more at a time. The father too had a job that required travel. The parents worked hard to keep their schedules complementing each other so that one parent would always be home. The maternal grandparents lived nearby and helped out if necessary. Bobby had an infant sister who was being cared for at the same daycare home he had attended.

The teachers had tried using stickers and rewards for self-control. It was clear that Bobby longed to please them but was overwhelmed from within by feelings that were too strong for his resolve. The parents felt bad about their son's behavior but did not know what to do for him. He was much the same at home and was especially jealous of the younger sister. They compromised their jobs to come for him early many days. The grandparents also came often to get him, as everyone felt a shorter school day might help.

When the parents learned of my availability they requested to meet with me. They were very concerned about their son and at a loss to know what made him so angry. The mother knew it was hard for Bobby to be away from her. She was torn over the financial need to provide family income, her own wish to develop her career, which was on the rise, and her wish to mother her son well. I learned the family was struggling to pay large medical bills incurred during Bobby's first year of life when he had been very ill. The father's income was modest and could not support the family and pay down this debt.

The mention of first-year illness was a clue I wished to follow up. Bobby's rages clearly demonstrated his inability to use loving feelings to contain and temper the rage he felt. This ability has its start during the first year of development, so the two facts went together in my mind. In order to use them to help Bobby and his parents, I needed more detail.

The parents told me of the hard start Bobby had had in life. Throughout the first four to five months of his life he had cried constantly, eaten voraciously, and vomited frequently in a violent fashion. Nothing had worked to calm him. The pediatrician had felt, since the infant did gain weight just within normal limits, that Bobby suffered from severe colic and would gradually improve. When this did not happen, at about four to five months of age the child was hospitalized for evaluation. Bobby underwent a barium-swallow X-ray several times. He was diagnosed to have a partial pyloric stenosis, which meant the valve between the stomach and intestine was very tiny and inelastic, so food could not pass through his system in a proper fashion. Much was vomited out. Surgery was required to correct this, and after it was performed the crying and vomiting stopped. Mother stayed with him at the hospital but was not allowed to be with him during some procedures. She was present for many blood drawings and IV installations. She became tearful as she told of these events and told of her horrible sense of helplessness to comfort her baby.

This vivid account of Bobby's traumatic experiences as an infant certainly seemed to explain at least part of his difficulty with keeping loving feelings dominant under stress. The mother continued to relate subsequent events, such as her return to work once Bobby was well and his placement at the daycare home. He had always objected to her leaving, so it was often father who dropped Bobby off at the sitter's. The grandparents would often pick him up early and would care for him when he was ill and not allowed to be with the other babies in care at the sitter's. When Bobby was 18 months old he was transferred to the current daycare in the toddler room.

He seemed to settle in quite comfortably at first, with his mother staying the first few days. Saying goodbye to Mother continued to be hard for Bobby, so once again Bobby said good-bye to Mother at home and was taken to daycare by Father. The stormy times described ensued. When Bobby was about two and a half his sister was born. He was both loving and jealous of her, especially during the first six weeks when mother stayed home with the infant while Bobby continued in his classroom.

At first the parents had the expectation that I would be able to tell them what to do in one or two sessions and their son would just stop this unreasonable behavior. As with the first parents described, I had to begin simply with educational information about the long process of development that takes place in children, and the central role of feelings. I learned that Bobby had a long-standing sleep disturbance which kept them all awake until late hours. Bobby could not stay in his own bed, and spent many nights in the parents' bed. I stressed that I could only make educated guesses at the beginning and that only by talking with Bobby about his feelings could he let us know the best way to proceed. This would be slow work. The parents agreed to meet weekly for a while to see if we could get to know each other and learn the best way to help Bobby.

We began with the ''goodbye'' trouble, which I felt was linked to the sleep problem. It was my idea that Bobby needed

Mother's care in particular because of the weakness of drive fusion (the ability to use loving feelings to temper anger). A child develops this capacity out of the reliable loving care given by the mother. The early medical trauma put this in jeopardy, and the placements in care subsequently further compromised its progression. The parents were astonished when Bobby eloquently told how lonely he was at school thinking of Mother. He sobbed with abandon. Mother could say how she missed him too, and was able to see that avoiding the scene at school did not help Bobby feel able to cope. She promised to be the one to bring Bobby each day and left her work telephone number for him to call her whenever he needed her. She arranged to talk daily with the teacher to keep in touch with events in class. This was both to help us identify what events triggered Bobby's rages and to build a closer working relationship between the mother and the teacher. Bobby responded to this attention to his feelings eagerly. He and mother had feelingful goodbyes at school and Bobby called to "touch base" with her when stress mounted at school. She called him daily just before naptime. Bobby became affectionate with his teacher and could allow her to help him calm more easily. At home the sleep trouble improved with regular bedtime routine. Bobby was no longer allowed in the parents' bed, but needed his bed to be in the next room rather than in his own upstairs room.

The changes in behavior and attitude were dramatic. The parents and school were delighted and felt all would be well from then on. The parents wanted to stop our meetings. I shared with them my opinion that we had only begun, but agreed to be available to them on an as-needed basis. This honeymoon period lasted for about four months. I then received a call: The classroom rages as well as tantrums at home were on the rise. When we met again it had become clear at school that Bobby could not tolerate situations where he felt he was not in charge of what would happen. At home he had similar difficulties around family routines and was especially difficult at bath and shampoo time. The mother was most upset over the shampoo situation, so we began there. She asked Bobby what was so hard about the shampoo. He felt he could not breathe and was choking. With this description from Bobby of the feelings that fit being forced to swallow the barium, I could advise the mother to tell him that it sounded like his body was remembering, at shampoo time, something that happened a long time ago, before he could talk. He had a sickness then that made it necessary for him to tip his head back and swallow medicine. He had fought and choked then and had been extremely frightened. Bobby then wanted to hear the story of his early medical experiences. I urged the mother to share the facts with Bobby, but to dwell mostly on how it felt to be so scared and helpless.

Once more Bobby's reaction was dramatic. He wanted to hear the story over and over, saying, "and I was so scared. I thought I would die" (the latter, his own addition). Also, "I wanted to punch them and kick them!" His mother told him he had done so, but the grownups were much bigger and stronger than he was and he could not make them stop. She told him how sorry she and Daddy and the doctors were to have to scare him so and make him so mad. He had been much too little to understand why and did not know any words yet to ask questions. They cried together over this story many times.

The progress of the work came in waves. Bobby seemed to concentrate first on the helpless feelings. He learned how to do his own shampoo and could use his teacher's help to curb feelings by saying such things as "This is only school," "You can boss yourself, but not others," and "We'll tell Mommy how hard it was to share the blocks or stop the play." His mother could keep in touch daily with both Bobby and his teacher. Bobby asked one day what the medicine tasted like, "Was it mint?" He had always gagged at the slightest hint of mint flavoring. Together they called the doctor's office and learned that indeed the barium was flavored with mint. Overlapping this work, the second wave centered on the anger stirred by helplessness. As Mother emphasized the good intentions of everyone in spite of the feelings roused and the seriousness of the illness Bobby had, he began to be able to give and accept apologies. His attention span and frustration tolerance improved as well.

Each new wave of work would be signaled by a regression in self-control. Mother and teachers came to recognize this signal and let Bobby know there must be a new worry on his mind. He became preoccupied with blood and bandages. From this they could discuss all the scary drawing of blood and the IV's Bobby had endured. They talked especially of how angry Bobby was at

Mother for allowing these procedures. It made him feel she did not love him. When he was in the grip of this feeling he lost track of his love for her and then he would lose all control until the feeling was spent. Mother helped him with this by sharing how awful it felt. She could tell him that no matter how mad he got at her, she loved him anyway. Most important, he needed to know that his own loving feelings would always come back. They had to live this scene painfully many times over, and his teacher needed to say these words as well as keep in frequent touch by telephone. Bobby could say he felt like such a bad boy to feel he hated Mommy. Gradually he gained in self-control and self-esteem and became proud of his social and academic abilities. He became a more confident child with a pleasant facial expression. The work was interrupted when the family needed to move out of town because of a job change. The mother was now able to read Bobby's behavior and he was much more in tune with himself. He now could use words instead of behavior most of the time. The parents know continued periods of stress lie ahead as Bobby works and reworks his difficulties. The process described took place over a two-year period and does not include the portions that had to do with ordinary developmental issues, which Bobby also brought to our attention.

It is important to note how the same themes keep coming up. This working and reworking of difficult sets of feelings allow for a gradual easing of tensions. Each go-around would bring some new subtlety and some new clarification. This is the nature of ongoing work, and it cannot be hurried. Perhaps you noticed also that the topics discussed were not chosen by me, but by the child's behavior. This too is a recognizable process that can be depended upon to show itself once a working relationship has been established.

UNDERSTANDING HOW FEELINGS ARE CONVEYED

It goes without saying that in order to "read a child's feeling messages" one needs to be well versed in the emotional tasks of each phase of child development, so as to know the most likely topics that would be on the child's mind. In addition, it is helpful to be able to recognize common ways a child chooses to act out his questions and concerns. For example, Bobby reenacted a feeling from the past in a current ordinary routine, his shampoo. Until the parents could separate the feelings from the shampoo and match them with the correct event, no sense could be made of his panic. They all simply felt helpless and enraged.

This telling of an unmasterable feeling by causing the feeling in caregivers is very common. The trouble is that usually the child simply gets punished rather than understood. Teachers are confronted with this often. It is important to become able to recognize that the feeling stirred is the message; the task is to set the parents thinking of what event could have caused their child to have that particular feeling. Another function of this acting out a feeling is to repeat the scene in as concrete a form as is available.

We all do this whenever any event, such as an accident, occurs that floods us with too much feeling. Repetition aims at taking the surprise out of the event by reliving it with advance knowledge, thereby attenuating the feeling. The hope is that after enough times of repeating the event, the feeling will be small enough to forget.

What gets in the way of recognizing the meanings of puzzling behaviors from children is usually the feelings of helplessness they create in adults. If one wishes to do meaningful work about understanding children, the most important person to have under control is oneself. I do not suggest that feelings of anger, disappointment, helplessness, frustration, and the like, should not occur, only that they need to be recognized and either set aside as an interference to understanding or used as important messages that need to be translated.

Just as the parents need to feel the teacher can "stand in their shoes" in order to trust and work, so do the parents need help to "stand in the shoes" of their troubled child in order to read his behavioral messages of distress. I hope the situations offered help clarify this process.

6

Thinking About Fathers

ERNA FURMAN

Many people appreciate the fact that young children are deeply affected by the loss of their father through death or family breakup. It causes not only temporary stress, but burdens the subsequent growth of their personalities and the helping task of the mothering person. Studies at the Cleveland Center for Research in Child Development have amply documented this (E. Furman, 1974, 1991; E. Furman and R. A. Furman, 1989; R. A. Furman, 1986). But what about youngsters who never had a relationship with their fathers, either never knew him or knew him so little as to never build a meaningful attachment?

Felicity was three and a half years old when her mother applied to the Hanna Perkins School, in part to provide a good educational experience for her daughter, and in part for help with some annoying habits, namely, Felicity's persistent thumb-sucking and her extreme demandingness. Since the mother had repeatedly expressed her disapproval of Felicity's thumb-sucking, especially in public, she experienced the child's persisting with it as highly provocative. Mother had even tried to bribe Felicity, promising special gifts for giving it up, but even this had proved unhelpful as it further exacerbated the little girl's constant demands. Despite her minimal means, the mother had always cared for and about Felicity devotedly and had made a special point of providing nice clothes, toys, and treats for her. However much these seemed to delight the child at first, they invariably proved unsatisfying after a while, and new demands ensued. Their arguments and hurt feelings over these issues had

79

become so intense and continuous that they left no room for mutual good times.

Felicity was a very pretty, competent, healthy girl, but she lacked self-confidence and was rarely pleased with herself and her good achievements. She lived with her mother but was also close with the nearby grandparents and wider family. The father was not in the picture. The child was conceived during a brief love affair which both parents viewed as temporary because the father was married, had several children, and did not intend to leave his family. The mother looked forward to raising her baby on her own. After an initial small support payment, the father moved to another state. The mother learned of his whereabouts indirectly but did not maintain contact. She never spoke to Felicity about the father, nor did Felicity ask. In fact, mother was sure Felicity had never even thought about a father. Through her work with the therapist, and with the help of the teachers' detailed observations, the mother gradually became aware that Felicity's unceasing demands were in fact disguised demands for her father, that the girl's dissatisfaction with herself and with all the things mother provided represented her disappointment at never getting the wished-for father, and that the thumb-sucking, too, indirectly conveyed the message, "Since you never give me the right thing, I'll give myself what I like and that'll show you up!" Mother even came to realize that, in her constant giving of things and great upset at being unable to satisfy her daughter, she was unknowingly responding to the child's unspoken ideas, had felt bad for not providing her with a father, and had acted as though lots of things could make up for this void.

Soon the mother decided to address Felicity's questions and feelings in words and to clarify sympathetically what she could and could not provide. Felicity responded with direct questions about her father, and mother told her the truth. They hugged each other and felt a new closeness in mutual understanding. Felicity's thumb-sucking and indiscriminate demandingness subsided, but she now wanted to get in touch with her father, painting pictures for him. Although the mother prepared Felicity for a likely disappointment, she did arrange to send the pictures to the father with a note to tell him of the child's wish to meet him. Much to their surprise, he responded and in time a meeting was arranged. As fathers often do, he succumbed to his little daughter's loving charm and, with mother present, they spent a good afternoon together. Felicity returned to school glowing with happiness and proudly showed the acorns and pinecones she had collected with "my real daddy." Although contact with the father remained sporadic and sometimes disappointing, the mere having and knowing her father proved a great boost to Felicity's self-esteem. Above all, the newly gained frank understanding between mother and child greatly improved their relationship, allowing them to share good times as well as to feel with each other during the disappointing times. Just as Felicity increasingly came to like herself as she was, so the mother, too, no longer felt vaguely guilty or defensive and could be more realistic in limiting her purchases of clothes and gifts to fit her means.

Felicity's story is, of course, individually unique, but we have witnessed a similar course of events with a number of our preschoolers. Moreover, we have noted the even younger children's intense interest and feelings about their absent fathers in our Mother-Toddler Group (E. Furman, 1992, 1993).

Ben's father had left the family before Ben's birth and had never seen his son, his only child. When some of the toddlers talked about their daddies planning to visit our Group, Ben's mother asked me privately whether grandfather could visit. I agreed but suggested she think about this with Ben first and prepare herself and him to answer other toddlers' questions about Ben's father. I knew from past experience that this might happen. The mother talked with Ben and with the therapist with whom she worked on Ben's behalf. At first Ben simply refused the offer of grandpa's visit. This surprised mother, but not me, because we had several toddlers who refused to accept visits from beloved grandfathers or uncles until their as yet unvoiced concerns about their own fathers were addressed. So it proved with Ben who, it turned out, had imagined that a neighbor was his dad, although he hardly knew the man. It took mother and child some time to clarify the reality, but after they did, Ben agreed to have his grandpa visit. As soon as he announced this at our snack time, the two-year-old girl sitting next to him asked, "Why not dad?" With mother's help, Ben could now explain that he did have a dad, but he lived far away and could not visit.

LISTENING IMPLIES RESPECT

Many mothers and caregivers are incredulous of such experiences. Working with toddler and preschool teachers in our community over many years, I usually hear initially that no child ever mentions an absent father, that all of them unquestioningly make Father's Day presents for various male relatives, that not having a father in the home is so common that all children accept it as a simple fact or do not even notice it. But after we have worked together for some time, after the teachers and caregivers have become more perceptive observers and learned more to listen to and respect their charges' thoughts and feelings, they increasingly report incidents that contradict their previously held convictions. Many of them then help the mothers to observe and listen, too, and assist them with understanding and feeling with their youngsters.

There was a time when we thought similarly that young children have no thoughts or feelings about sexual matters or about death. We have learned that children indeed do not voice their questions and concerns when they sense the adults would not welcome them, but do so very readily when they can trust to be heard and understood (Herzog, 1980; McDonald, 1963; E. Furman, 1978a; this volume, Chapter 9). However hard or painful the realities, the children and their relationships are invariably helped when their loved ones can respectfully clarify their concerns and empathize with their feelings. There is, after all, no child without a father, and knowing about or longing for one's own appears to be part of our givens. I recall working in a residential institution many years ago where one little four-year-old not only did not know his father, but had truly never known a man. All staff were single females, and there were no male visitors. He surprised us with his grandiose tales about his big, powerful and wonderful father and his assumption that this person was the mailman whom he had seen drop off the mail, but whom he had never actually met.

In working with teenage mothers especially, I tend to encounter not only their difficulty in listening to their children's ideas about their father but their own unwillingness to allow him a role with the child and dismissal of him as a person, often accompanied by anger at his lack of financial support and characterological shortcomings. There are many good reasons for their attitude, but they do not seem to take into account that this unqualified exclusion and denigration of the father affects their children. Can a child trust that mother will respect him or her when she so utterly disrespects their father? Can a son feel valuable and valued in growing up to be a man? Can a daughter learn that men are not mere sex objects and should be considered for their positives, along with acknowledgment of their negatives?

I know there are no easy answers to these human dilemmas, but respecting our children's thoughts and feelings has much to do with respecting ourselves and with building a community in which we all learn to respect one another. Respect, like charity, begins at home.

7

Mothers, Toddlers, and Care

ERNA FURMAN

The goal of this chapter is to explore the stresses and dangers that substitute mothering may pose to a toddler's personality development, and to discuss whether we can minimize them and how to go about it. With this in mind we shall first remind ourselves what a toddler actually is, describe the main developmental tasks he or she has to master, and discuss the factors that facilitate healthy development during this phase, focusing especially on the most crucial factor, namely, the role of the mother-toddler relationship. We shall then explore ways in which substitute mothering may affect the primary mother-child bond, what happens when substitute mothering overtaxes the mother's and child's tolerance for the stress and interferes with development, and, last, how we can adapt substitute mothering to lessen the inherent stresses and perhaps avoid ill effects.

WHAT IS A TODDLER?

A toddler toddles. He is mobile; he is on the go. He can choose to stay with us, to leave us, to come back. This characterizes the state of the toddler's development as a person. Unlike the younger baby who cannot, of his own accord, leave the mothering person literally and who also mentally can hardly exist without her as a person, the toddler has begun to view self and mother as separate people.

The behavioral hallmarks of the toddler's beginning development of the self are his wish and ability to take over some of his care, to meet some of his own needs. The baby begins to become a toddler when he can feed himself, with fingers, cup, and spoon; when he can, to an extent, comfort himself and make himself feel good, by using a part of his own body, such as thumb-sucking, and by using a "transitional object" (Winnicott, 1953), a blankie or soft toy that he has made his very own, because it links him to mother and bridges the gap between them; and when he can recognize and dislike pain and discomfort, can protest, can make them known to his mothering person and seek and accept comfort from her, saying, though not in all these words, "I am hurting, I don't like it, I want you to know and I trust you to make it better." The toddler not only wants to do for himself what he already can do (pushes away mother's arm when she tries to feed him or refuses to open his mouth for her spoon-feeding, screams and struggles at being picked up when he can walk, and later yells, "Don't carry me."). He also wants to do for himself a host of things that he cannot yet do so well or that mother does not trust him to do well—be it getting the cookie box off the shelf, turning on the water faucets, crossing the street. The unrelenting zest for "me do, me by myself" provides enormous pleasure, especially when it leads to mastery, and also brings anger and frustration when it is interfered with.

At the same time mother has begun to matter as a person. The older baby recognizes her as different from everyone else and thinks about and looks for her mainly when a need arises. When he gets closer to being a toddler, mother's part in meeting his needs is so special that he often foregoes need fulfillment when she cannot minister to him, even when others do it in much the same way—does not want to eat, or go to sleep, or be cleaned up or "kissed better" when she does not do it with him. This means the infant has reached that crucial developmental point when the relationship with the person has begun to be more important than the way his needs are met. Now mother's companionship, their social interactions and feelings for each other are *the* thing. Everything mother does with her toddler means a lot, and he observes everything she does without him and wants to do it with her and like her, cooking, cleaning, talking on the telephone. He even *stops* doing some things or does them *her* way for the sake of keeping her love and for the pleasure of becoming like her. At the same time, her presence and her good feeling for him are necessary to sustain his zest for independence, his wish to do for himself and even his wish to get away and to turn to others for additional fun, to Dad and siblings and other family members. When she is not there, the harbor is gone and venturing out feels less safe and less fun. Without her, the toddler's activity becomes less purposeful and his achievements may crumble.

Not surprisingly, toddlers often want to leave mother or send her away, but do not want *her* to leave *them*. Yet, for stretches of time and under favorable circumstances, toddlers can keep mother in mind during her absence and can keep their feelings for her and with her. This enables them to relate to a mother substitute and to maintain their own personality achievements during limited periods of separation.

It takes a lot of healthy mental and physical endowment on the child's part and a lot of good mothering on the mother's part to grow from a baby into a toddler. We usually see significant indications of this developmental achievement by the first half of the second year.

THE MAIN DEVELOPMENTAl TASKS OF THE TODDLER PHASE

We often say of a thriving child, "He's all put together." In the case of a toddler this describes very aptly that he is succeeding in the business of putting his self together, body and soul. This implies not only that he develops the many new functions, activities and skills we shall enumerate, but that he comes to know them and to enjoy them, that he values them and makes them his very own, fits them together and uses them for purposeful functioning, for coping with himself and his world, and for interacting with others. It is not enough when a toddler knows how to walk and to manipulate things with his hands. He has to enjoy his motor control, has to make it a precious part of his "me," and has to want to use it for himself, be it to run to mother or push her away, to retrieve his teddy, to put on his shoes, to make his way in the world. It is only when a toddler can invest and use all these parts of himself that they can afford him satisfaction, and it is only when he can integrate them into a coherent idea of self, of "me," that they can contribute to his self-esteem. To be "put together" means not only that one thinks of oneself and functions as a whole person, but also that one likes oneself. A toddler who develops a sense of self and of self-esteem is a person who is "with it," a person who has zest and initiative, a will to master, and has fun as well as pride in doing so. We can tell him from a compliant automaton who does what he is made to do, from the chronically contrary ill-humored child who *only* wants to do the opposite, and from the incompetent, bewildered child who responds to most situations by feeling overwhelmed and helplessly falls apart.

Among the many new personality parts the toddler has to develop and encompass are the use of large and small muscles for effective motor control, the use of language for thinking and purposeful communication, a grasp of the outer outline of his body, of where it begins and ends, including the parts he cannot see, such as his behind (when toddlers first learn to wipe themselves they usually aim for the general area but later, when their behind has really become part of their body concept, they manage to touch the exact place). And because he likes his body, he learns to avoid common dangers and shows or tells his caretakers about specific discomforts, a scratch or bruise or sore ear, and solicits their help. He even extends his sense of ownership to his clothes and possessions, recognizes, treasures, and looks out for them. He also gets to know what goes on inside his body, differentiates his needs and knows what to do about them, to eat when hungry, to sleep when tired, to control elimination. A wish for and mastery of self-care become manifest in proficient self-feeding, in considerable accomplishments in self-dressing and washing, in falling asleep on his own, and in independent toileting. He makes most important strides in the area of feelings which are no longer simply pleasurable or unpleasurable sensations, but become more subtly varied and modulated, and which are no longer only discharged bodily, but experienced mentally and increasingly recognized, tolerated, even named and shared in words—happy, mad, lonely, excited, sad, envious, bad, good. Along with these steps we see new interests in play, such as blocks and tricycles, rhymes and songs, which serve to practice skills, and dress-up and role play which serve to differentiate himself from others, to interact with them and to "put himself in their shoes," to try out how it feels to be like them.

This brings us to another aspect of the toddler's personality development, namely, the new and different way he relates to his mother and the tasks he has to accomplish in the context of this relationship. The toddler's lack of consideration for others is well known, as he grabs things from other youngsters and even steps on them to reach something or to go somewhere. Equally well known is his unattenuated intense mixture of love and aggression for those closest to him, especially his mother. Both feelings manifest themselves together in his aggressive hugs and in the twinkle in his eye when he teases and torments her; each is expressed alternately when he lovingly cuddles her one moment and attacks and rages at her the next, or when he angrily sends her away and wants to exchange her for a better mommy, perhaps over just a minor frustration. These characteristics do not change of themselves. The hallmark of the toddler's achievement is to tame and tone down his raw aggression and to overcome his self-centeredness for the sake of mutual love. He learns to maintain his loving feelings and loyalty in spite of disappointments, to transform his rage into anger and to express it without harming his loved one. In doing so the toddler brings about a real change in the nature of his impulses, in his ability to tolerate frustrations, and in self-control. At the same time this makes his relationships more stable and consistent, makes him more considerate, and paves the way for new and more mature relationships with peers and adults. Most important, it enables him to take into himself admired aspects of the parent's personality and thereby to enrich his own. A toddler who has taken this step masters his toileting because he wants to be clean the way his mother is and is pleased with himself when he is like her. Having made cleanliness into his own valued thing, he will extend it to his possessions, his room, his schoolwork, his job, and take pride in it. A toddler who has not taken this step may become toilet-trained, but his achievement will not add to his self-esteem, is apt to be unreliable and easily subject to regression under stress. He is not likely to extend cleanliness to other areas and will consider cleaning up as a nasty chore at best. Cleanliness will not be truly his own. This ability to take in attitudes and ideals through a relationship and to make them a permanent part of one's own self is crucial for later learning, for character development and effective conscience formation. Without it, all such gains tend to be unstable; what is there one day may be lost the next, or enables him to function in one setting but not in another.

WHAT DOES THE TODDLER'S PERSONALITY DEVELOPMENT DEPEND ON?

Obviously it depends on many factors, such as good health, an adequate bodily and intellectual endowment, reasonable stability in his physical environment, space and safety to be active in it, and a large measure of good luck. Above all, however, his development depends on a continuous enough and good enough relationship with the mothering person who has helped him to become a toddler in the first place.[1] This relationship is the crucial facilitating factor. It does not mean that the mother needs to be perfect or that she should actually be with her toddler every minute. It means that she thinks of herself as his mother always and feels responsible for his well-being at all times, even when she is not with him. It means that she has invested herself in him as a part of herself and as her loved person. This special ongoing inner bond with her toddler usually enables her to gauge whether and when he is ready to be without her, with whom and for how long, how he feels and copes when he is away from her, how to reunite with him, and how to bridge the gap of separation by sharing their mutual feelings and individual experiences, what they did and what all happened. If, during a separation, the child cannot keep his inner tie with the mother, he cannot continue to make developmental gains and may lose what he had already acquired. If the mother cannot maintain her inner tie with her toddler, she may lose her capacity to progress in her maternal development, may get stuck at relating to him at the current level and fail to appreciate his changing needs. For example, we often see that a mother who is with her toddler only at night continues to care for him as if he were an infant. She may even regress in

---

[1] The "mother" in the context of all chapters is the mothering person or primary caretaker, not necessarily the biological parent.

her mothering ability and lose touch with her child and, in extreme cases, may cease to function as a mother with him. Even their physical reunion may not serve him or her to reestablish the vital link. For example, one day at her daycare center a child suddenly bit Mary's arm. She made no response. Even when her careworker, who happened to see the incident, rushed over to comfort her, Mary remained completely impassive. At pickup time, when the caseworker told Mary's parent, showed her the toothmarks, and apologized, Mary remained expressionless, while the parent remarked, ''Well, she used to bite so I guess it serves her right.'' The parent had lost her feelings for and with the child, just as Mary had lost her own.

Mothering is not a given. The ability to enter the developmental phase of parenthood (E. Furman, 1969b) and to progress adequately as a parent depends in no small measure on the ongoing mutual interactions with the growing child. The child's response to the mother and their physical togetherness is almost as important to the mother's development as it is to the child's. Klaus and Kennell's (1976) work has highlighted the value of postnatal contact with the baby for the mother's ''bonding.'' But this holds true not only for the first few days. All mothers need to be with their infants and care for them actively to get their mothering under way and to achieve that special stable investment in the child which enables them to help their child grow and to grow with him, and to maintain their mothering ability during separations. Mothers vary in how much togetherness, caring, and interaction they require to facilitate their maternal development; they vary in how long it takes them and in the extent to which separations from the child endanger it. For most mothers, however, the child's toddler phase is still a vulnerable period during which insufficient opportunity for ongoing active mothering may interfere in the nature and consistency of their ability to parent effectively and cause lasting damage to its further development. We tend to be more aware of the child's need of his mother than of the almost equally important mother's need of her child to assure harmonious growth. I am not implying that being with the child is the only factor in maternal development or that other factors cannot seriously impede it, but wish to stress that it is a crucial, often neglected factor and one we need to keep in mind especially in considering the role and effects of substitute mothering for young children.

I also wish to stress that the concept of a mother's stable investment in her child, the hallmark of mothering, has nothing to do with the currently fashionable term ''quality care vs. quantity care.'' Being ''all there'' for the child at certain times, at times especially set aside for that purpose, is a most desirable attitude in those who maintain additional relationships with a young child, such as fathers, grandmothers, babysitters, or at a later time, teachers. They fulfill their function by being fully invested in their role with the child at specified times, but can essentially go about their own business at other times. Not so with mothering. Its quality depends on the uninterrupted mental investment which is always there and enables the mothering person to feel with her child regardless of whether she is with him or away from him. It enables her to wake up and attend to him, though not necessarily cheerfully, at night when he is sick, to drop everything in the kitchen and charge after him into the living room, though not necessarily with a smile, because she sensed an ominous silence which told her he was in trouble, or to feel a twinge of regret and pain when she watches him march off happily on a drugstore expedition with Dad while she stays behind to go about her business on her own.

WHAT AFFECTS THE MOTHER'S AND TODDLER'S ABILITY TO MAINTAIN THEIR RELATIONSHIP DURING SEPARATIONS?

Experiences in working with mothers and caretakers of infants and toddlers suggest that the following factors contribute significantly. The list is not exhaustive and does not explore their interaction, nor does it attempt to describe the additional effect of events and circumstances in the past and present lives of the mother-child couple, such as illnesses, family constellations, socioeconomic conditions, births and deaths of other family members, or even the relative emotional health of mother, child, and their relationship. I shall focus specifically on those factors that are directly connected with the mother's, toddler's, and caregiver's handling of temporary separations.

First, there is the time factor: How often do the separations occur, how long do they last, and do they include periods of bodily need fulfillment? Mothers and toddlers generally tolerate best separations of a couple of hours in the morning or afternoon, during periods when the toddler is awake and active and does not need to be fed, bathed, dressed, go to sleep or wake up. In other words, when his body is under least stress and his mind functions optimally.

Then there is the place factor: Does the toddler remain in his home during the separation or does he stay elsewhere? And if he stays elsewhere, does the place resemble his home, is it a totally different kind of setting, is he fully familiar with it? And, especially, has the mother been with her toddler in this other place long enough and in such a way that she has experienced everything and everyone there with him, so that he can rely on her full knowledge of him in it and so that she has a complete mental picture of all that happens there with him? And, similarly, is *he* familiar with where *she* is and what she does there (visited her place of work, for example) so that he can picture her in her surroundings? Obviously, it is easier for a child to maintain his concept of self and of mother when he remains in his home, and progressively harder the less homelike the setting is and the less familiar he is with it. Similarly, the more intimately mother and child are acquainted with one another's whereabouts and activities, the easier it is for them to maintain the mutual link and to bridge the gap of separation after reunion.

The factor of shared preparation for the separation and followup after it, is important too in that it helps both partners to master the separation. Sudden and unexpected leavings of each other, without a transition period of leave-taking, and uncertain times of reunion are quite stressful. Many of us know how poorly children react to the mother's "disappearance" and how badly they tolerate her absence when it has no predictable end. We can similarly remind ourselves of how distressed, frantic, and furious a mother is when she has unexpectedly lost sight of her child, when he perhaps "disappeared" behind the counter in the department store or when father or an older sibling takes him along on an errand without letting her know.

This brings us to the factor of who is with the child during the separation. Is it someone mother and toddler both know well, someone with whom they have both shared togetherness, some-one who has learned how they are with each other and who therefore carries the trust of their togetherness and becomes a constant reminder of it? And does this person actually receive the toddler from the mother and hand him back to her? This, of course, makes it easiest for mother and child and obtains most often when the child is cared for by a member of the family or by someone in a similarly close relationship with both. Maintaining mental contact with each other becomes much more difficult, even impossible, when the caretaker is relatively or totally un-known to mother or child, when the mother does not personally participate in the transfer of the child to and from the caretaker, or when the child goes from one caretaker to another or even a third one during the separation period. For example, toddlers are often brought to a center by a relative, handed over to an early-duty caretaker, then go on to someone else to join their group, are switched to a next person during nap to allow for the regular caretaker's ''break,'' and, on a late day, are transferred to another special group or are picked up by another family member with whom they stay until mother gets home.

Equally important is the factor, ''Does mother stay in charge?'' Do mother and child take it for granted that the tempo-rary substitute cares for him at her direction, that she knows about and has sanctioned everything the substitute does with him and the way she does it? Is she called upon to decide what and how things are to be done if there is something unusual (''Would you like Jimmy to wear his snowsuit today?'' ''Do you want him to go outside yet after his recent cold?''). Does the caretaker report to her what the child did or said and what happened while she was away, and does the mother inform the caretaker of partic-ular events or circumstances that occurred, how they may have affected the child, and how the caretaker could help him with them, be it a family upheaval, or his tummy ache the previous night, or a car accident witnessed on the way? When mother remains responsibly in charge, when the caretaker works at her behest and under her direction, the mother-child tie is much safer for both partners than when she hands over her child, in mind as well as in body, and lets others do for him as they see fit and does not even get to know just how they go about his care. Unlike the older schoolchild, the toddler can only share with mother those parts of his life that she already knows. This is not only important in the case of employed sitters or caretakers, nor does it concern only ''bad'' things that the substitute may do to him or with him. It applies just as much to family members and to things they do which the child may like very much but which go against mother's wishes and/or are not cleared with her, for example, staying up late, eating certain foods, playing games or watching TV programs that are usually off limits, to mention but a few of the more harmless indulgences. If the mother has not okayed these things, happy ones and unhappy ones, they inevitably burden and threaten the mother-child relationship and affect the role it has to play.

This brings us to the last, but by no means least, factor, the attitude of the caretaker. Does he or she do mother's jobs without taking her place? And does he or she build and use the relationship with the child in such a way as to help mother and child maintain their vital link? This is the hardest part of being a good substitute—to be at one's best by accepting oneself as second best. Early on in my professional training Anna Freud told us that a good child psychoanalyst keeps in mind, feels with and deals with, three facets: the child, the mother, and the mother-child relationship. This applies even more to being a good mother substitute, especially with a young child. The caretaker's helpful attitude shows itself in so many ways: she understands and supports the child's thinking and feeling for the mother during the latter's absence and reminds him of her when he seems to have to shut her out from his mind or seems in danger of forgetting about her; she accepts the child's complaints when she does not come up to par in her handling, does not do as well as mother does; and when she does things that seem to him more fun than what mother does, she reminds him that Mom wanted him to have that fun while she was gone and that they will tell her about it so that she can share in it; when the child welcomes mother on her return, the good sitter accepts being dismissed and when he teases mother on her return, keeps her waiting and wants to do one more thing with the sitter, she tells mother and child that he probably missed Mom a lot and wants to give her a taste of how hard it is to wait for someone we love, that that matters really more than the extra game with the sitter, and that, anyway, it is really time to be with Mom now. It is a difficult task to be a good sitter, especially when the mother is very far from perfect and when the child is very loving with us. It is hard then to remember that his ability to be so nice with us stems from his relationship with his very imperfect mother. Without that he could not relate to a substitute at all.

A substitute cannot help mother and child to maintain their relationship when she does not have a relationship with each of them herself and is not in feeling touch with them, when she does not know the mother or does not consider her maternal needs, or when she cannot adequately relate with the child, perhaps because she has too many children to look after or because she is only geared to meeting his bodily needs. A substitute also cannot fulfill her true task when she views herself as the mother, be it in the sense of being the child's second mother or even of being his primary mother. This happens in daycare when it considers itself the "home away from home" or sometimes assumes that it is actually the child's primary home because he spends so much of his day there. It happens even more frequently when the mother substitute is a family member or resident caretaker in the home, a father or grandmother who regularly shares in the toddler's care, or a nanny or housekeeper. Caretakers who take over as mothers usually invest themselves very intensely in the child and feel very close and loving toward him, but they leave out the mother and the child's relationship with her, or compete with her for the child. They handle the child their own way, may even feel they do a better job of it. They do not keep the mother in close touch with what they do and with what the child experiences while he is with them, do not readily follow her directions and wishes, and do not support the child's thinking and feeling for his mother during her absence, but often welcome his apparent lack of response to being away from mother. And when the child states a preference for being with them, they see it as a good sign of his fondness for them rather than as a danger signal of the child's difficulty with loyalty, difficulty in dealing with his anger at mother, and difficulty in maintaining his vital relationship with her. Double mothering is very different from substitute mothering, and poses its own special threats to the primary mother-child relationship.

WHAT HAPPENS WHEN SEPARATIONS BETWEEN MOTHER AND TODDLER OVERTAX THEIR TOLERANCE AND ADVERSELY AFFECT THEIR RELATIONSHIP?

In the normal course of development toddlers seek out familiar people, enjoy new and special activities with them, and form meaningful relationships with them which are maintained in addition to, not instead of, the primary relationship with the mothering person. Prompted by their as yet unresolved mixed feelings about their mother, toddlers often also seek out or wish for others to be new and better mommies, the proverbial better bread and butter at the Joneses. Sensible mothers and ''others'' do not allow this actually to happen because they realize that, far from helping the child, it would interfere in his task of coming to terms with his dissatisfactions with his own mother and with the reality of his situation. In the normal course of development, however, there also inevitably arise circumstances in which the mother has to arrange for substitute care during limited periods, at least for such occasions as her own doctor's appointments, an older child's school conference, or a special shopping trip. If these separations are helpfully managed, they are good learning experiences, times when mother and child can test and practice their means of coping. Masterable stresses may serve to build mental ''muscles.'' By contrast, extended, repeated separations of mother and toddler tend to become unmasterable stresses for one or both partners and endanger the mother-toddler relationship and the personality growth that depends on it, especially if they involve double mothering, multiple mothering, or unhelpful substitute mothering.

These kinds of interferences are not new or newly prevalent. They are not limited to this country or to specific socioeconomic groups. The very affluent in all countries always employed caretakers for their children and still do so; the very poor have always left them with family members or neighbors out of necessity, while mothers helped with farming or later, with industrialization, flocked into factories. Wars and the ravages of epidemics and of economic hardship have always disrupted family lives and mother-child relationships (Tate and Ammerman, 1979; Thomas, 1977). Historic exhibits in one of South Carolina's plantations show pictures of the slaves' day nurseries, a big room supervised by a black daycare worker with many little mats on the floor, each occupied by an infant. This is how the slaves' children spent their days while their mothers were at work, some no doubt providing double mothering for "the master's" children. All slave cultures were run on similar lines through the ages. And the extended families in many culture patterns fall far short of the imagined ideal we tend to attribute to them. Not only do they involve double and multiple mothering, but youngsters are often dropped off at a moment's notice with relatives or friends whom the child does not know, just as in this country children are sometimes sent to grandparents far away who are close with the mother but near strangers to the child. Indeed, early extended separations and substitute care are not new or limited. What is new is our efforts to understand their effects.

To my knowledge the first scientific inquiry originated with Anna Freud and her co-workers. In Vienna, during the years of extreme depression which followed the first world war, she ran a daycare center for toddlers from deprived families. It was called the Edith Jackson Creche, named after the generous American colleague who financed it. The toddlers' day there started with a bath in the early morning. Later, during World War II, Anna Freud and Dorothy Burlingham ran The Hampstead Nurseries in London. They cared for infants, toddlers, and preschoolers who were separated from their families to protect their lives during the blitz bombardments and to enable their mothers to participate in the work of the war effort. Again American generosity helped out and the now famous descriptions of Anna Freud's and Burlingham's (1943, 1944) findings originated for the most part with the monthly reports to the fundgivers, among them this country's Foster Parents Association. Shortly after the War it was again Anna Freud who was sought to consult with Israeli mental health professionals and educators. They had noted some of the distressing effects on many children raised in kibutzim in which extended substitute parenting was the rule. More recently, other studies have become available, among them the study of English daycare by Bain and Barnett (1980) and in the U.S.A. the related publications by White (1978) and Provence, Naylor, and Patterson (1977). Among the developmental interferences stressed in these studies are delays and deficits in language development, both during the toddler phase and during the later school years, especially difficulties in using speech for comprehension and communication. Also noted, at the time and in later schooling, are increased aggressive manifestations and difficulty in impulse control. Those who have mainly studied schoolchildren, in followup, find a prominent tendency to learning problems, characterized by academic performance below intellectual potential; lack of motivation; difficulties in concentration, in ability to invest and enjoy interests and activities and in integrating and using what has been learned. Bain and Barnett also point to ''damage or severe interferences in personality development.''

My experiences with care of infants and toddlers have taken several forms. They began in the forties, when I cared for youngsters in residential settings, and became an ongoing focus of interest for me during the last 20 years. My most detailed data have been gained from the psychoanalytic treatment of five school-aged children who had experienced substitute care or double mothering in their earliest years. With each seen in individual sessions five times weekly for about four years, their symptoms and personality functioning could be unraveled and traced to their origins. Their early care experiences proved to be important causative factors in their pathology (E. Furman, 1967). Another source of detailed data was several preschoolers with emotional difficulties who had similar early care experiences and who attended the Hanna Perkins Therapeutic Nursery School. Observations at the school and weekly sessions of treatment via the parent for two to three years enabled us again to relate some of the children's troubles to the effects of earlier care. My colleagues at Hanna Perkins and at our Center's child-analytic clinic also worked with such cases. Through our regular scientific meetings, I had a chance to compare data and to extend and confirm findings. At the same time my regular consulting work with daycare centers afforded an opportunity to learn how toddlers, mothers, and careworkers respond to these experiences at the time when they are actually taking place, and to apply the understanding gained through therapy in the form of preventive educational measures. This work began with my participation in the Home Start Project, a family daycare program under the auspices of the then Cleveland Day Nursery Association. In more recent years our CCRCD responded to community need by offering an ongoing yearly course, ''Toddlers in Daycare,'' which I have taught and learned from. In this course directors and careworkers from about ten daycare centers for toddlers and infants meet with me every other week to discuss the children's development, educational practices, contacts with parents, individual youngsters' difficulties and ways of helping them.

What, then, has it been possible to learn? First of all, it is noteworthy that the observations of toddlers' and mothers' responses to various forms of care confirm the retrospective knowledge gained from the therapeutic work with older children. The personality difficulties that are seen to underlie the older children's problems can be observed as they take shape during toddlerhood, and they manifestly interfere with the toddler's mastery of his developmental tasks even before they contribute to his trouble with later ones. For example, the toddler's difficulty in developing his valued independent self-concept may show in not wanting to take over care of his body, while the older child's similar difficulty interferes with his self-motivation in learning, prevents him from making his learning his own thing and from investing his interests and activities.

Although even during the toddler's process of development a variety of factors interact to produce an interference, it is often possible to pinpoint the effect of substitute care when we can alter it to mitigate the stress and observe the child's responses to such a change. For example, we have noted repeatedly that toddlers who neither recognized nor cared about their own and others' property in a daycare setting, began to treasure their own and respect others' belongings, including the Center's toys and equipment, after they were encouraged to keep one of their mothers' belongings (a scarf, a glove, a coat) which they could carry with them or deposit wherever and whenever they wished to, without anyone interfering. This measure was one of several designed to help the child maintain his inner tie with his mother and his self. Such instances helped substantiate the link between the effects of care on toddlers and on later development. Treatment of some of the older children with trouble in caring for and respecting property revealed a connection with early care experiences, but it was by then harder to isolate this factor from others which had early on and subsequently contributed.

In contrast to other studies which tend to single out several specific areas of difficulty in connection with early care, our findings suggest that any or all areas of personality development may be affected, but especially all those we have listed as the developmental tasks of the toddler phase and which, as such, form the basis for later growth. This, we must remind ourselves, includes not only many aspects of the development of self and self-esteem, but particularly the ability to form and maintain stable *caring* relationships.

Obviously, not all children suffer or suffer equally. No two individual experiences or personalities are alike, but a sufficient number of them manifest problems or interferences in development to indicate that there is a risk for all.

CAN WE ADAPT "CARE" FOR TODDLERS TO AVOID ILL EFFECTS?

The insights gained from therapy and years of work with gifted and dedicated caregivers in our course are consistent with national professional standards for toddler care. They have enabled us to develop many approaches and measures that have lessened the stress sufficiently for some toddlers to overcome difficulties and have perhaps helped others to avoid potential troubles. We have not been able to follow the children long enough or closely enough to know whether all ill effects were avoided. We do know that bringing about the many changes in attitudes and procedures which we use is difficult. It makes many demands on the mothers and caregivers, but it also brings them many pleasures and satisfactions and a greater sense of shared effort.

The onus falls on the caregiver. If she is a person who truly enjoys toddlers and feels in tune with them (which, by the way, is very different from being good at relating with preschoolers), she can probably also learn to feel with and understand all the things we have just discussed: when a toddler really is a toddler and can relate to a substitute, what his developmental tasks are, what the mother-toddler relationship is about and the role it plays, how separation may affect this relationship and the many factors that help to bridge the gap during absences. Above all she will appreciate that she is a substitute, that her role with the mother is to help her realize her importance, that her role with the child is to help him maintain his relationship with his mother and to do so in a setting that meets his developmental needs. Given that, she will find the many practical ways that serve to put this attitude into practice. I shall mention a few such practical measures, but want to stress that they work only when they are used within an overall helpful context, not when they are isolated gimmicks.

An initial interview with the mother and her visit of the care center in session, without her child, first serve to listen to her, to get an idea of her expectations and of her understanding of what substitute care will mean to her and her child, and to ascertain whether he has mastered the pre-toddler developmental steps. This helps to gauge how best to introduce to her the realities—that her relationship with her child is and needs to remain the most important part of his life, that their separation will inevitably put a stress on this, that the caregiver's main task will be to help her child to keep his mom in his mind and in his heart but that she, the mother, will also need to participate, to help him with his feelings and to cope with his responses which may show in unwelcome ways, like contrariness or sleep troubles or regression in toileting, and that, to start with, she will need to free up time to help him with the new experience. This will take at least one or two weeks during which she will be attending with her toddler, starting with an hour or so and gradually extending it to the full period. This will give her a chance to know fully all that happens while he is there and, especially, to get to know his caregiver so that all three of them can begin to relate and trust one another. One skilled director reports that mothers' initial reactions range from "Oh God!" to "No problem" or even "I like that." It is never easy to work out the necessary schedule. Many a letter is sent to mothers' employers to enlist their cooperation, sometimes by telling them that a mother's comfort in settling in her child helps her ease of mind at work and ultimately makes her a better employee. Most mothers do manage to participate fully and effectively, enjoy being truly welcomed and involved and, after the separation is effected, use many ways of keeping in touch—joining the child for lunch, phoning at certain times, picking him up early whenever possible, accepting and sharing feelings. Many mothers also find ways of shortening the separation period in order, for example, to assure that the child's stay will not exceed his caretaker's work hours and he will not need to be cared for by an additional substitute.

The caregiver uses the introductory period to understand the mother-child relationship, their ways of being and doing things together and to learn their language (all caregivers are multilingual because, in addition to special family words for special things, each toddler speaks his own language in words and behavior which usually only his mother really understands). As mother begins to leave, the caregivers main job starts, picking up, supporting, and verbalizing the child's feelings about mother's absence and return. It is very difficult for toddlers to sustain feelings without their mothers, not only feelings about her, though this is the first step. When they are helped to recognize and tolerate their angry, sad, lonely feelings about mother, it helps them to keep the tie with her and to build a relationship with the substitute, and this in turn helps them to tolerate and share feelings about other things, be it a current pain or an event at home. Without help with feelings the toddler survives, but does not function as a person. For some time children may only be able to feel when mother arrives; for example, one caregiver noticed that a rather new little boy kept touching his ear. Although his face was bland, she surmised he might be in pain. She told him so, telephoned his mother, and he accepted silently her comforting lap. As soon as his mother walked in he ran to her, clung to her, and burst into tears. It turned out he had a painful ear infection. This boy could recognize and feel discomfort and seek help, but not yet with a substitute. When mother and caregiver tell one another of the child's experiences with them, each can help the child maintain his appropriate feelings and make them a part of his continuous self. Mother helps similarly by talking about the caregiver at home and supporting his missing feelings about her, especially during holiday breaks or when the worker is ill. Remembrance tokens, such as little toys, from the center to home are a useful concrete link.

A steady rhythm of daily and weekly activities helps youngsters to gauge when to expect mother's return as well as the leaving of the center for the weekend. It develops their sense of time and helps them master the changes; for example, ''Now it's lunch, then it's rest, then it's music, then Mommy comes,' or ''Today is washday, then is take-home-your bags day, then is weekend-stay-at home day." Transitions from and to mother are the hardest times for everyone. They are the times when loyalty conflicts and stored up feelings on the child's part surface, and when tensions between mother and caregiver about their respective roles with the child become most touchy. Good caregivers look out for these times and help and support the mother when she is "on the spot." When little Janie had a spell of really giving her mother the business at pickup time, the caregiver did not take over and do it "better," did not pretend to ignore it, did not even just stand by and watch. She caught the runaway Janie at the door and handed her over, then called mother up in the evening and said, "I am sorry that Janie still shows in this way how much she missed you. She really makes it very awkward for you. How would you best like me to help at these times? Let's think it through together and work out a plan."

When mothers feel in charge and respected, they also respect the caretaker, watch and learn from her ways of handling children, ask for advice, want to share concerns and talk them over. These are not opportunities for posing as the "expert," but for listening, for sharing what "other mothers sometimes do" or what "we have found helpful at the center," or, if necessary, for paving the way toward suggesting professional assistance, preferably with someone directly or indirectly connected with the center.

But what about the care setting, its equipment and opportunities for intellectual stimulation? One then-new member of our course who was planning to open a new daycare facility asked for suggestions for toys and apparatus. The experienced caregivers were unanimous. "Ask your mother and aunts and neighbors for all their spare kitchen and household utensils, their pots and pans and plastic containers, their old spools and jar tops. That's what you will really need." They were basically right. Create as homelike an atmosphere as possible and help the toddler explore and understand his world which is the home. His best "field trips" are the kitchen, the laundry, the broom closet; let him do things there, if at all possible. Toys and materials are best introduced singly and slowly, in keeping with individual children's readiness and the caregiver's ability to play and do with them. It is through the shared pleasure of the loved one that skills and activities gain lasting investment. This brings us to the most important aspect of the "curriculum": have as few children as possible to one adult. After all, a mothering person has her hands full with one toddler, just because he needs all of her.

We can tell that a youngster is mastering the stress of substitute care when he pursues his developmental tasks with zest and self-motivation and enjoys his achievements with his loved ones, with the mother and with the mother substitute.

WHAT ABOUT MOTHERS WHO HAVE GREAT DIFFICULTY IN MOTHERING, DIFFICULTY IN FEELING WITH THEIR CHILDREN, DIFFICULTY IN HELPING THEM WITH DEVELOPMENTAL STEPS?

Obviously we cannot change people nor can we serve everyone. We can only do our best to help those who want to work with us. "Our best" in such cases, however, is not to focus on the child and give up on the mother or to discount her importance for the child. The more tenuous and burdened the mother-child relationship is, the more important it is for the substitute to help the toddler maintain it and to underline its positives. A mother who has even just managed to help her child live to be a toddler, must have devoted a considerable amount of effort and care to the task, prepared many meals, changed many diapers, got up many nights. In some such cases the most helpful approach is to admit mother and child to the center, support her care for him there, and let her help with and join in the activities. A number of mothers could in this way be helped to feel worthwhile and invest their children more lovingly.

PART II

8

On Toilet Mastery

ROBERT A. FURMAN, M.D.

In this chapter, I propose the use of the term "toilet mastery" in lieu of the standard expression "toilet training." Toilet mastery more accurately delineates the psychological tasks involved in obtaining cleanliness and dryness, better integrates the various methods that facilitate the process and, further, points the way to approaches in the first year that can helpfully pave the way for its successful acquisition. It is a phrase derived from pediatric practice of over 30 years ago, but one that has proven helpful in psychoanalytic practice and teaching. It is a phrase that may follow in the spirit of what Friedlander (1946) was addressing in seeking "on the basis of . . . theoretical considerations practical advice [that] can be given to mothers . . . on how to achieve the training for cleanliness so as to guarantee the most positive character development" (pp. 346–347). This is of concern to child analysts who consult with pediatricians, with daycare staff, to analysts who have in analysis mothers of toddlers or who consult with such mothers.

In the spirit of Friedlander's remarks I shall want to integrate theoretical considerations about the toddler phase of development with the very practical questions of how children can best be helped to become clean and dry. It is a developmental area where the theoretical and the pragmatic blend well together. In pursuing this goal I shall trace the evolution of my thinking as the path I trod has, I believe, been followed by many before and since, without, to the best of my knowledge, anyone having explicitly described or reported on the full journey.

LEARNING ABOUT TOILET TRAINING

My own personal analysis began at the same time as my pediatric residency, and my analysis and my analytic and psychiatric training overlapped for some of the five years I was in pediatric practice. During my pediatric residency my analysis stimulated my interest in understanding more of the anal phase of development, wondering how it manifested in toddlers, how one could help mothers to help their children through this phase most successfully. I remember listening in vain in my residency for any enlightenment from my teachers. Finally, in a conference when the question was pertinent to a case under discussion, I asked a respected senior practicing pediatrician how he managed helping mothers to get children clean and dry. In full seriousness, he responded that he waited until the children were four and then asked how training had gone. "They've almost all made it by then," he explained. Undaunted, I pursued the same question with the man I most respected as a practitioner. He was puzzled by my question, saying that mothers just never seemed to ask him anything about that.

I went into practice armed only with what I had learned in my analysis and what I had gleaned from Spock's (1946) then most popular book, which at the time I felt to be weakest in this particular area, though helpful in so many others. I did with this problem what I had learned to do about breast-feeding: ask the mothers who seemed most successful. As I was picking up bits of information from some mothers, word seemed to spread within my practice that this pediatrician would talk about toilet training, and I found many previously silent mothers asking for advice, telling me of their apprehensions and of what felt to them as prior failures. That toilet training is a concern of mothers was emphasized by a section in a delightful book called *The Complete Book of Absolutely Perfect Baby and Child Care* (Smith, 1957). In writing about toilet training, the author invoked her cardinal rule for mothers: "Lie! Lie to your mother, lie to your sisters and aunts, and above all, lie to all the other mothers you meet on the street. When a newer mother than you asks for your help, tell her you never had the least trouble" (p. 25).

What I want to describe first are the "gimmicks" I collected that seemed to facilitate toilet training. There is no pejorative in my designation as each in its time and in its way was helpful. It is just that this is the best way to characterize my level of understanding at that juncture. Some of these I learned from mothers, some from my teacher, Dr. Anny Katan, some from colleagues such as Elizabeth Daunton and my wife, Erna Furman, and some from sources I can no longer identify.

The first thing I went after was encouraging mothers to register some disgust after bowel movements and wet diapers when their children were getting close to two. I marveled at how some very successful mothers could automatically not register disgust when changing a three-month-old, but then, almost simultaneously, register some mild but clear displeasure with a two-year-old sibling who was wet or soiled. Only later was I to learn what counts is what a mother feels and communicates spontaneously, not what she tries to act out at her pediatrician's behest.

Next I went after diapers, sensing that no child could comprehend his mother's exhortation to be clean and dry if she kept him in diapers, acting as if she did not expect that he could achieve that goal. This pursuit led me to see that in those flash seconds when a toddler has recognized that elimination is about to happen, getting to mother to get diapers off to get to the potty in time is just not going to work. I began to stress the use of training pants and easy-off boxer shorts, or easy-off overalls.

Where to put the excrement came next, and I became a proponent of the potty or potty chair, one to each floor of the house, to try to avoid the fears that some toddlers had of the regular toilet or of those contraptions that go on the regular toilet and that are so hard to get to and look as if they would not feel like a safe place to sit. Dr. Katan was helpful with the suggestion of the use of newspaper in the corner of the bathroom for those who seemed too afraid of the potty, not to mention the toilet or special toilet seat.

By this time I was becoming aware that more and more I was heading to having the child be able to take care of things on his own, not always requiring his mother's assistance, either with clothes or with access to a suitable receptacle. Unfortunately, this dawning awareness did not lead to true insight yet, but did lead to talking with the child about what was going on and what it was that mother expected. It is hard to believe I came to a mother's talking with her toddler so late in the evolution of my thinking, but such was the case. Even more surprising were the mothers who had not particularly talked with their child before, and toilet training for some marked the beginning of communicative speech.

Talking about training led next to the question of when: At what age should training start? This in turn led to a number of other considerations. I first fell back on what I had learned about weaning, to encourage mothers to look for the child's signals that he is ready, helping them to identify what those signals might be—dryness through nap time, sometimes even through the night; interest in what went on in the bathroom; some signs of beginning disgust with dirty or wet diapers. These signs came much earlier than many mothers seemed to be willing to acknowledge, say from 16 months on, and the mothers with difficulties observing these signs comprised the group that steadfastly hoped the child would ''train himself.'' There were many reports usually available in the community of children who had trained themselves, and these always fascinated me. Some of these reports I felt I could document as coming from mothers who followed Mrs. Smith's dictum. In most other instances there were slightly older siblings or neighbor children at work. No one can come down more vigorously on an untrained toddler than a two-and-a-half or three- or three-and-a-half-year-old who has just achieved dryness and cleanliness. His newly acquired maturity is at risk of regression in the presence of untrained, apparently unconcerned, playmates; ''You stink'' is a mild expletive for some of the older ones to use with their untrained younger siblings or playmates. Dr. Anny Katan pointed out that some incidents of ''self-training'' result from fear, provoked in many ways, one of which might be the toddler's observation of a fierce toileting struggle between mother and an older sibling.

Another group that intrigued me were the babies reported as fully trained by a year of age or thereabouts. A mother who had achieved this remarkable feat explained to me that as soon as a baby can sit, one starts training by looking for the moment when elimination is about to occur. She felt a cool potty on a warm baby buttock could then initiate the reflex emptying of the bladder or rectum. She explained that if such a regime is conscientiously followed, there would be no more dirty diapers by a year of age, save, of course, for nighttime. This mother never could accept my feeling it was she and not the child who was trained, even after brief absences from her toddler would totally end the child's cleanliness.

The question of when then led to another consideration: when in a developmental as opposed to a chronological sense? I was struck one day with the report a mother gave of her twenty-month-old daughter on the potty while the mother was simultaneously giving the bottle to and changing the diaper of her eight-month-old son. The little girl found a rubber nipple on the floor and placed it in front of her privates and called her mother's attention to her accomplishment with apparent glee. Obviously here was a child trying to deal all at once with the pushes of three usually successive developmental phases: oral, anal, phallic. This seemed a bit unfair for the little girl. In dealing with her, the mother had hardly known what issue to address first, and so had said nothing, though she had observed well. I was also struck with the number of children who would be signaling their interest in becoming clean and dry and would still be on the bottle, as well as those children described by Galenson and Roiphe (1980), who in the midst of their toddlerhood were being grossly overstimulated in the phallic sense.

I could reason out that one developmental conflict at a time seemed the most fair and reasonable approach, and this analytic concept was one that many mothers could quickly and most helpfully grasp. It was helpful in the sense they could more deligently pursue bathroom privacy, discuss with me the pros and cons of training by showing as opposed to talking, and could hustle along with a weaning they might have been a bit sluggish to allow to be completed. The relevance here of E. Furman's (1982) paper, "Mothers Have to Be There to Be Left," should be all too clear in that some mothers have a reluctance to respond to their infant's signals of wanting to wean because it makes a mother feel too much like being left by her child.

At this point I had all of my "gimmicks" in place and could embark on a reasonable discussion of toilet training with the mothers in my practice: one phase at a time, so get weaning done as well as privacy in place; watch for his or her signals; talk about what lies ahead; no diapers—rather training pants and easy-off clothing; no toilet seats—potties or potty chairs instead in each bathroom. I could also leaven this discussion with quotations from Mrs. Smith's book.

These thoughts were helpful to many mothers, but what was so striking to me was that some mothers went their own way with no help from me and did just fine, while some mothers seemed to follow my thoughts to the letter and got nowhere. This was the next puzzle I had to face: what made the difference so that my advice was valuable for some, the same advice useless for others?

TOILET TRAINING VERSUS TOILET MASTERY

At this point I had to become the observer, and this is where for the first time I felt I was having fun in my pursuit of understanding, the pleasure of a slowly dawning insight. The best simile I know has to do with words and music, with my "gimmicks" like the words, the mother's attitude like the music. When the words were combined with the right music, things went well; without the right music they were of little value; it was the music that was crucial, and it was possible to observe what that music was. Some mothers worked *with* their children, helping them to acquire cleanliness and dryness; this was the right music. Other mothers, by contrast, were doing something *to* their children, getting the children to do something mother wanted. From this insight was born the concept of assisting a child to achieve toilet mastery by working with him, as opposed to toilet-training the child, doing something to him. At this point the gimmicks could make sense in that, if used with the proper music in the proper context, almost all of them were geared to helping the child achieve mastery of his elimination.

What is crucial here is how much a pediatrician can assist a mother in stimulating as well as supporting a child's wish to be big, to be grown-up, to progress in his development. To the extent this wish is active in the child, the mother can ally herself with the part of her child that wants to be clean and dry, and support him in his struggle with his urges to mess and stay dirty. In other words, mothers can be helped to make the child's developmental conflict an internal one within the child, not an external one with her.

Many years ago our neighbors had a particularly charming, towheaded toddler, Billy, who was, if anything, perhaps just a bit too placid and passive. One summer day, from over the hedge separating our lots, came from Billy a totally out of character, resounding "No!" Our guess that toilet training had just started was easily verified. Unfortunately, an external conflict had begun. Seeking toilet mastery, as opposed to imposing toilet training, cannot, of course, eliminate all of the externalized conflicts, but they can be greatly modified as the goal is pursued of developing the wish to be clean and dry and then allying oneself with the child's wish.

I am not certain how "oppositional" a toddler has to become to emerge fully as a separate and individuated person. This chapter is not meant to address the entire range of emotional development in the second year, just the acquisition of toilet mastery.[1] A few observations would, however, seem germane. My experience confirmed what Anna Freud (1963) said, in speaking of the mother's role: "If she succeeds in remaining sensitive to the child's needs and . . . identified with them . . . , toilet training will proceed gradually, uneventfully, and without upheavals"(p. 254). I am certain that "oppositional" behavior that focuses on the toilet-training process all too readily can slip into an unhealthy tug-of-war struggle which benefits neither the acquisition of drive mastery nor of drive fusion, i.e., the ability to tame anger with the help of loving feelings. I would also venture that the teasing of his parents a toddler does in his age- and phase-appropriate way of relating offers adequate scope both for any "oppositional" behavior he may need and the arena needed for its successful management and containment.

Not only did the concept of toilet mastery allow integration into a coherent whole of the many otherwise isolated bits of advice or suggestions, it also allowed focus on some psychoanalytic principles that were meaningful to parents and, further, pointed the way to many steps a mother could encourage during the earlier phases of development that could ultimately facilitate acquisition of toilet mastery.

Toilet mastery, incidentally, was a term first used in the fifties in child development lectures for medical students. I first

---

[1]For a comprehensive study of toddlers' personality development see E. Furman (1992, 1993).

used it in a scientific paper in 1975. I fear I came upon the term
as a description of an observed phenomenon rather than as a
consciously derived psychoanalytic concept dealing with drive
mastery. But it is clear that the term described the mastery of
the drive for pleasure in dirt and messing by use of a reaction
formation by which the young ego is able to turn the drive into
its opposite, a wish for cleanliness and dryness. It is a term that
puts cleanliness in its proper context as a means and not as an
end, as the arena in which developmental progression and phase
mastery slowly evolve with all their attendant personality
achievements.

To my pleasure I found that many mothers could readily
understand reaction formation, "turning an urge into its opposite," and could understand the contrast with the earlier ego-
drive relationship of the oral phase, where weaning and self-
feeding involved diverting an urge into a slightly altered form
of gratification. I learned from these exchanges with mothers to
look a bit more closely at how mothers responded to their baby's
first purposeful thumb-sucking at around three months to note if
they could derive pleasure from the baby's satisfying of an urge
without her participation. One learns a great deal about a mother-
child relationship with such observations and can, I believe, at
least plant the seed with some mothers of the pleasure they can
enjoy in observing and facilitating an infant's acts of mastery.
With mothers who announced to me at the start of my work with
them as a pediatrician that they dreaded toilet training—and there
were a surprising number of mothers who did so spontaneously
or in response to a general questioning of what their future concerns might be—I would discuss thumb-sucking, self-feeding,
weaning, in terms of mastery of urges, important preliminary
steps to the mastery involved in getting clean and dry.

THE MOTHER AS LOVING FACILITATOR

I felt these discussions about urges and mastery did something
more for many mothers if they could encourage them to observe
their infants for clues as to developmental needs and progression,
to see their role as the loving facilitator, as Winnicott (1965)
would say. Such an attitude intrigues and encourages many an

apprehensive mother and is something a pediatrician can actively encourage and support.

I was always impressed how one could discuss in nonscientific terms, free of jargon, almost any psychoanalytic concept with mothers of very young children and what they in turn could add that was helpful to my thinking. One of my favorite examples is of the mother in the office nursing a small one of a few months in front of her toddler who seemed to tolerate the experience quite well. I asked what the toddler thought of the nursing, and the mother explained that she thought the older one had been afraid the baby was eating her, having no chance to see the milk that was the issue of the transaction. She had first put this into words for the older one and then had expressed some milk into her hand for him to see, explaining that he too had been a baby, before he had grown big enough to eat foods at the table like Mommy and Daddy.

I interject this anecdote to point to another area where mothers can be of assistance before toilet mastery acquisition actually starts, and that is with drive fusion, the taming of anger through love which is a prerequisite for the availability of the neutral energy necessary for personality tasks. I have always felt that ''a good feed,'' as the British would say, promotes drive fusion, as angry and loving feelings in their earliest manifestations are unavoidably combined in the act of sucking, just as, one might add, they are in the acts of elimination. More definitely, as reaction formation involves not just the turning around from pleasure in messing and dirt to the pleasure in cleanliness, but also the switch from cruelty to pity, that which facilitates the one will facilitate the other. In preparing mothers to look for signs of readiness to wean I would suggest, among other things, that they watch for biting of the nipple if breast-feeding, biting of the rubber nipple if bottle-feeding. It is not a bad question to ask mothers of five- or six-month-old babies what they would do if they had their choice, if bitten while nursing, a question that easily follows in the context of thinking ahead about the signs indicating readiness for weaning. Some mothers have anticipated the situation with the thought that, like many others they have heard about, they would bite back, a remedy they have heard is most effective. Advance discussion to curb reflex reaction was surprisingly helpful in stimulating a more controlled and helpful response of a natural show of pain and verbal explanation: it hurts Mommy and is really not something the baby wants to do, that is, hurt Mommy.

The thought not unnaturally leads to talking to a baby, again something the pediatrician can easily ask about and encourage from day one for mothers and fathers, stressing that speech is going to be such a help for so many different forms of mastery, something that only comes from being talked with. If a pediatrician declares early on an interest in talking with a child, he is going to learn of some very remarkable and fascinating conversations of all types that many mothers have, even with their preverbal infants.

As precursors of drive mastery, drive fusion, reaction formation, verbalization, all can have their beginnings in the first year so, of course, it is true that the healthier the mother-infant relationship is in the first year, the easier becomes the task of acquisition of toilet mastery within the context of that relationship. A question I want to raise here is really a psychoanalytic one of what personality attributes are acquired as a consequence of that mastery, and which attributes are necessary prerequisites to being able to achieve mastery. I am suggesting that many helpful aspects of the small child's relationship to his drives can be started on the path to mastery long before beginning the tasks involved in becoming clean and dry, and can significantly facilitate the acquisition of an autonomous mastery of elimination. The slow, steady process of achievement of mastery solidifies and integrates this new level of ascendancy of the ego over the drives.

Even 30 years ago there were many mothers who asked when they could leave their infants and go back to work part-time or full-time. Focus on the relationship between mother and child as a vehicle for later toilet mastery often put this in a readily understandable context for many mothers: one of the goals of a successful first year being to prepare for successful passage through the tasks of toilet mastery, requiring the mother's presence and support. From this can emerge a developmentally based timetable in considering and weighing the factors involved in when a mother returns to work and for how long.

In talking about the acquisition of mastery with their toddlers, there were some key phrases I learned from my wife and supported mothers using: first, in anticipation of starting the process, "Soon you'll start learning how to be clean and dry (like Mommy or Daddy, or Sister or Brother)"; later, when the process was just under way, "Why didn't you tell me before?" and "Soon you'll be able to tell me before." The latter phrases help mothers at the outset of the acquisition of toilet mastery when toddlers show their first recognition of the process by coming to mother with their wet or dirty training pants. This focuses on the fact that toilet mastery takes much time, as will any process of true mastery.

These phrases allow another focus, and that is on the intellectual task involved in acquiring toilet mastery, a beginning of a time sense. What a mother is supporting in her child is becoming aware of a state that exists before something happens, encouraging the child to sense from the bladder or rectum signals that elimination is about to occur, and to do something before that happens into the training pants. This intellectual task helps a child in delineating his body ego by reading its signals correctly (Shengold, 1985). This intellectual task is difficult for the mildly mentally retarded and, if the retardation has not been picked up prior to beginning the work toward toilet mastery, both mother and child can embark on a task that is doomed to failure and disappointment for each. This task should start on a developmental timetable, not a chronological timetable. This is something learned through 15 years of consulting at the Mental Development Center of Case Western Reserve University where it was so strikingly unusual to find a mildly retarded child without the stigmata of an unfortunately premature and unsuccessful struggle to acquire toilet mastery. There are other factors involved here, of course, such as the wish of mothers of mildly retarded that their child be clean and acceptable even if retarded, but it is this factor that then takes priority over recognition of the intellectual requirements of this developmental step.

THE PEDIATRICIAN'S ROLE

In the past I have shared these thoughts with pediatric residents whose outpatient pediatric practices have been in the well-baby clinics of inner city hospitals. The response has often been,

"Well, that must have been very possible in an affluent suburban practice, but it will never help me with the mothers I'm seeing." The residents have a point but not, I believe, the one they think they are making. My practice experience came from three years in a suburban area that was not really affluent and from two years in the Air Force, where we dealt with the dependents who could not afford the locally available excellent civilian pediatric care. What is the point, however, is that in both my situations the opportunity was there over time to form relationships with the mothers that make such pediatric work possible, something usually so absent for pediatric residents in their all-too-short one- or two-month assignments to pediatric outpatient facilities.

In my practice, what was also striking to me was that if I had an agenda, an outlook, a philosophy about the pediatrician's role, it quickly became known in the community and, as it repelled some who wanted nothing of this approach, so it attracted others, a surprising number of others, who were intrigued by its possibilities, mothers who spanned all socioeconomic groups.

A final word about a pediatrician's agenda as manifested in a general approach as well as in concrete suggestions to help a mother help her child achieve toilet mastery: what is crucial is the mother's attitude of assisting her child with his wish for cleanliness at the time of his developmental readiness, a wish of his she can do much to facilitate. The concrete suggestions, such as about timing and potties and training pants, are of secondary importance to a mother's feelingful in-tuneness with her child. But these suggestions are not insignificant as they can concretely exemplify and illustrate to a mother what the process is all about, which also can facilitate an identification for the mother. Likewise, the place and ways these suggestions fail or are misused provide the pediatrician with insight into and ability to pinpoint the locale of the problems of some mothers within themselves.

IN CONCLUSION

The purpose of this chapter has been to introduce the term "toilet mastery" as a scientifically sound term to describe a mother's facilitation of her toddler's acquisition of dryness and cleanliness. Focus on toilet mastery in lieu of toilet training properly pinpoints the personality task for the toddler, one that opens the way to measures in the first year that can helpfully prepare a child for the task and underlines for professionals the complex personality ingredients involved in successful passage through this developmental phase. In purely pragmatic terms, focus on "toilet mastery" can assist mothers more successfully in facilitating their child's negotiation of this period of development.

We have here, I believe, something of a paradox in that the acquisition of autonomous dryness and cleanliness should not be the end point of the anal phase of development as much as it should be the means by which the personality has achieved another step, a most significant step, in its gradual ascendancy over instinctual drives.

9

Plant a Potato—Learn About Life (and Death)

ERNA FURMAN

It was the end of June, almost the last class of our Mother-Toddler Group before the summer vacation (E. Furman, 1992, 1993). It was the day we harvested our potatoes. Each child had planted a potato in early April, had marveled at the dark-leaved vines that grew out of seemingly nowhere, and puzzled over the strange little flowers that appeared on them. Now everyone crowded around our 1' × 8' vegetable plot in the playground. When the first toddler dug in deep with my help, pushed aside the plant, and turned up a bunch of small potatoes dangling from its roots, there were surprised "Ah's" and "Oh's" from the mothers and children. None of them had really expected potatoes to grow. Not a single mother or toddler had ever seen potatoes being planted or dug up, and even planting them, watching them grow, and talking about it had not prepared them for the outcome. Only now, digging, groping for the potatoes in the earth and pulling them out one by one, did it "click." Suddenly they recalled the different growth stages, voiced their earlier doubts and misunderstandings ("I thought they'd hang from the vines," said one mother), and rejoiced at being able to put together all the sequences and make sense of them as a whole. Now they could even think and ask about "What comes next?"; "Do you throw away the vines?"; "Will it have more potatoes if we put earth back on them?"; "Can we plant the little potatoes and grow more potatoes?" I explained that the vines would die and I would then dig them into our plot to make good earth for new plantings.

This last step in the cycle was readily understood because we had had many earlier experiences with it throughout the school year. All went home proudly carrying their few potatoes, planning how they could cook and eat them, and feeling happily content, the way one feels when one has truly understood something and made it one's own—beginning, middle, and end.

For me too the last step in the potato-growing project was the most familiar, but for a different reason. Helping youngsters to understand the end of living, death, is the task I had started with many years ago. At that time my colleagues and I had learned from our work with bereaved children that coping with death depends on first knowing what dead means (E. Furman, 1974, 1978a). A basic concept of death is best grasped not when a loved one dies, but in situations of minimal emotional significance, such as with dead insects or worms. Since all children encounter such deaths very often and since even toddlers notice and ask about them, we can help them by utilizing their experiences and interest instead of averting our or their eyes. Dead means the lasting end to signs of life. When a fly no longer moves, eats, drinks, or feels pain, it is dead. In working with young children we have consistently used such opportunities to help them understand what dead means. They, more often than not, have in turn taught us that they already knew that the dead fly would not live again when they suggested that we dispose of its dead body by throwing it in the trash. Soon they also alerted us to their observations of flowers and plants. These also live and die. When the flowers in our table vase wilted, they commented on their changed appearance and smell and asked us to "pitch them out." When our spider plant had some brown leaves, some said, "Look, it's dead. My Mommy had a dead plant and she threw it out with the garbage." They had no idea, however, where trash ends up beyond the garbage truck, and were intrigued with our practice of burying dead plant material in our little garden plot. Looking at the fallen leaves in various stages of decay helped them see how they turn into humus. Of course, the toddlers were equally intrigued with the little weeds and mushrooms that sprouted out of this humus and with the blossoms and leaves that grew out of the forsythia branches we had brought in on an unusually warm January day. Right away, they wanted to know whether we would bury them in the garden after they die. In short, they helped us appreciate that learning about death implies learning about life, and not just about the beginnings and endings, but about the generational sequence of the life cycle, "Can I plant my potato to grow more potatoes?"

EXPERIENCING THE LIVING AND DYING OF PLANTS

Picking up on the children's comments, we realized that plants were indeed the most prevalent, accessible, and emotionally neutral opportunities to learn about life and death, and we began to include them more deliberately in our curriculum. Starting our academic year in late fall when, in our climate, nature outdoors provides mainly for observations of death and decay, we introduced a sweet potato and, with the help of three toothpicks, suspended it half-way in a jar filled with water. Most mothers and toddlers knew sweet potatoes from the supermarket, some had eaten them, but none had seen them grow. Watching the tiny rootlets grow into a thick network and then the little purplish sprouting stems unfold into a big crown of trailing vines preoccupied us during many snack times, as each mother and child inspected the latest changes and carefully passed it on to the next.

We also began to look out for orange and grapefruit seeds, and planted them in little pots and watered them. But since these seeds grow slowly and turn into respectable little trees to be taken home only toward the end of the year, we first used popcorn (also one of our snack foods) for quicker results. Before the winter break, we set aside a few corns from our shelled cobs and, instead of roasting and eating, each child planted them in a little plastic container. Watering and caring for their popcorn during the holiday week provided a daily activity, a helpful way of keeping teachers and peers in mind, and produced a big lush green crop of stalks. On their return, some reported on their gardening success with glowing pride, some brought their pots in like trophies.

Everyone wanted to grow more things. And we did. We cut off the tops of our snack carrots and watched them grow their green lacy leaves in just a shallow dish of water. We grew beans in little jars with cotton. Forsythia and pussy willow branches not only flourished when forced in an indoor vase, but grew roots and were much in demand for later outdoor planting at home. We shook the seeds out of pinecones and planted them. Hardware and grocery stores donated big batches of outdated flower and vegetable seed packages which gave us a chance to compare many kinds of seeds. Some youngsters brought in mother's potatoes and onions which had sprouted long shoots in their storage bags. And in March, with the snow still swirling around us more often than not, we dug up our tiny plot, planted green onion bulbs (a great snack treat later on, chopped and mixed with cream cheese), then peas (which produced a lush crop, with mothers barely able to let their toddlers do the first picking and tasting because for most mothers it was also their first experience), and finally potatoes. As well, everyone planted his or her own little pot of flower seeds (mostly marigolds) to take home for the summer. Often, on meeting with the mothers and ex-toddlers again in the fall during their start of nursery school, the first thing they happily tell about is their flowers, "We put them around the house and they are all blooming!"—"Boy, did my marigolds get big!"

The successes of planting and growing are, all along, matched by experiences with failure and decay. Even the best sweet potato plant dies off and rots within a few months and some sweet potatoes do not even get started and rot very quickly. These lessons are sometimes harder for the mothers than for the children. Having noted the demise of one of our sweet potatoes, we buried it in our plot. The energetic little digger's mother said, "Now it is sleeping there, nice and cozy." Her little boy looked confused and I had to help, saying that he, Mommy, and I knew it was really dead. Mom caught herself and agreed. Not all beans, popcorns, or seeds grow, and some grow much taller than others. These are valuable lessons too. Popcorn grown in winter dies off and cannot mature because we cannot plant it outside. Why? What does it get outdoors?—another valuable lesson. Yes, there are disappointments, but they are manageable when they are discussed as part of the natural order of things rather than personal insults, and most youngsters are willing to give it a second, even third try—and, of course, we always have plenty of extra seeds or bulbs available for them.

THINKING ABOUT A LIFE CYCLE CURRICULUM

So what is new? Haven't many preschool teachers always had plants in their classrooms? Haven't they always brought in and welcomed their pupils' bringing in flowers? Haven't they always used seeds for making collages and for planting? Haven't they grown beans and sweet potatoes and perhaps even hyacinths in jars or peas and chives outdoors? Of course they have, and what we offer our youngsters is not new but perhaps different. How?

The first difference lies in the educational goal. Learning to plant seeds, appreciate flowers, or watch plants grow, each comprises a worthwhile but isolated experience. The focus in our curriculum is on the whole life cycle and, whenever possible, on its generational sequence. This approach has helped our youngsters to understand better life and death and the connection between them. We note the toddlers' considerably increased respect for and appreciation of life in their interest in and care for living things; for example, mushrooms are not thoughtlessly or intentionally trampled on, but noticed with the happy enthusiasm of discovery and gently protected from being harmed; flowers—even weeds—are not just torn off and then perhaps forgotten or discarded, but are left to grow and observed repeatedly for changes. The same interest and care are extended to even the tiniest animals, the pillbugs and worms, the spiders and gnats. In this context, death is observed with understanding and even a measure of pity, rather than ignored or treated as scary or exciting or even to be willfully inflicted; for example, "Oh, look what's happened to the carrot tops! Oh, too bad. Is it time to bury them in the garden?"; "Oh, look at this bug. It doesn't move. Is it dead?" Also, the children increasingly report on their other encounters with death—the "poor" little bird found frozen in the snow, the "poor" squirrel dead by the side of the road.

Of course, in helping toddlers and preschoolers develop this kind of thoughtful appreciation, growing potatoes represents merely the complex last link in a whole year's chain of experiences. Beginning with plants that grow fast and in full view is crucial (sweet potato, carrot tops, pussy willow), as is the progression to those that still grow fast but with a hidden-from-view state (popcorn, green onions). Even when these experiences have been integrated and the children are prepared to understand plant growth that is slower and invisible for longer, items need to be selected carefully. They have to be a familiar part of the child's daily life (peas, potatoes), have to grow well more often than not, and, preferably, will bear the seeds for a second growing cycle (peas, potatoes). Among the flowers, marigolds are particularly suitable because they grow readily, are insect-repellent, which keeps them healthy, and produce many seeds. The progressive selection also needs to be adapted to local conditions, such as climate and school setting, and, not least, to the children's capacity to integrate the successive experiences which may vary from group to group and which only the teacher can gauge.

Another aspect best gauged by the teacher is when, how, and how much to extend and link the learning about plants to other areas of the curriculum. This may include pictures of plants, flowers, gardens, markets, or books, such as *The Carrot Seed* (Krauss, 1945). Our youngsters have also especially enjoyed sketching and easel-painting of the plants and flower bouquets in our room. Some have mainly matched the right colors; others have produced surprisingly representational pictures. This extension was actually introduced by a two-and-a-half-year-old who one day decided on her own to paint a picture of our vase with daffodils. Others followed suit. On that occasion, as so often, once an interest is sparked, the children themselves carry it into other areas of activity and we, the teachers, learn from them.

THE PARENTS: A CRITICAL INGREDIENT

A second difference is the involvement of the parents. Although our toddlers' mothers come from very varied socioeconomic and racial backgrounds and although most of them have plants in their homes or even back yards, their unfamiliarity with the growth of their daily food items is as striking as their discomfort with signs of death. They not only expected potatoes to hang from the vines but, in many cases, had never seen peas flower and grow pods and did not know that pussy willow branch roots. Although they readily threw away plants or killed insects, they were squeamish about discussing this and tended to react either with disgust or denial, for example, the nice and cozy sleeping potato. Participating with their children in our life cycle projects stimulates *their* interest, helps them tolerate and understand these phenomena, and enables them, often for the first time ever, to adopt a more realistic and comfortable way of dealing with the minor daily encounters with death. This makes it possible for them not only to share and support their child's learning at school, but to extend it into the home—a vital step in helping the child to solidify and integrate what he has learned at school, and in assuring that his learning will remain with him and continue even when he no longer attends classes.

The teacher's efforts at linking home and school fail with the very young unless mother's enthusiasm matches her child's. It makes the difference between popcorn being watched and tended during the holiday week or allowed to dry up and die, between the little marigold seedlings being transplanted around the yard and lovingly cultivated or forgetting about them. As the mothers' interest grows and their qualms are allayed, they are eager to take home extra seeds to plant, repeat school projects at home, bring in flowers to identify and questions about their home plants. They report on outings to nearby farms and want to share their experiences and some of the fruit or vegetables they purchased. Fathers join in too and sometimes find their youngsters joining them, so that a father's gardening hobby turns from a time away from the family into a fun shared activity. A toddler's lesson may become a family interest. Having followed our toddlers' development in later years, we have learned that these interests often continue to flourish. We sometimes hear of new projects they have embarked on and sometimes of old ones that were kept up, ''You know my grapefruit seeds? Well, I have two big trees now, *so* tall!'' Of course, it is easier to foster parental enthusiasm when the mother attends classes with her toddler, but even when this is not the case, individual teacher-parent exchanges at the start and end of the day as well as scheduled conferences and group meetings with the parents can be used to share these aspects of the curriculum and to engage their investment in them. How effective such efforts are depends a lot on the teacher.

THE TEACHER: LOVER OF LIFE AND LEARNING

This brings me to the third and last difference I wish to stress, namely, the attitude of the teacher. If ''learning about the life cycle'' is merely a mandatory item on her curriculum, something she has to teach and has to get the parents to participate in, it will not work. The crucial ingredients are a teacher's own enjoyment of it, her feel for living things and respectful acceptance of the ways nature works, as well as her appreciation of the children's readiness and pleasure in sharing the learning with them. She does not need to be an expert, does not need to know all the answers. The children and parents respond to her attitude much more than to the facts she conveys. Wondering at and puzzling about the why's and how's of life's order and finding satisfaction in figuring out as much as one can is what it is all about.

Not long ago we tried three sweet potatoes in succession, and each failed to grow. We did not know why. Finally, inquiries revealed that potatoes are sometimes treated to delay or prevent sprouting in order to extend their marketability. I had not intended to teach these complications, but all were fascinated and understood when I shared what I had learned. It helped us to find a potato that would grow, and when it did, we had gained from the experience more than we would have from a first successful try. The teacher's ability to tolerate not knowing, patience in trying over and over again and, in this case, ultimately understanding cause and effect were a more important part of the experience than the healthy growth of the last potato. Whenever we have the chance to share with children and parents a mutual interest we really care about and can work with them toward a better understanding of it, there is deep satisfaction for us as well as almost certain benefit for them. Our work on the life cycle has indeed been most enjoyable and rewarding for us as teachers and has forged a special bond with the children and parents. And we are, of course, very pleased with all that the children and parents have learned and the pleasure it gives them.

KNOWING THE LIFE CYCLE: AN EMOTIONAL AND INTELLECTUAL BASIC

The teacher's attitude, the children's readiness, and the parents' involvement do not, however, of themselves account for the especially meaningful experience of this work for all participants or for the self-perpetuating way in which it continues to remain a part of the children's and parents' lives, remembering all about it, prompting them to expand on it and learn more in subsequent years. Working with preschoolers and kindergarteners at the Hanna Perkins School, but especially working with the youngest ones (roughly 18–36 months) in our Mother-Toddler Group, we have become increasingly aware that for learning to make sense, to provide a usable base of knowledge and to motivate further learning, it has to encompass not only whole beginning-to-end experiences, but especially those that help a child to understand his immediate world and prepare him to find his own place in it.

In our technologically complex and highly specialized society, many daily experiences seem like magic and defy true understanding for child and adult. Pushing the knob to turn on the TV or pressing computer buttons to get a mathematical answer are intriguing and efficient, but explain nothing about the workings of these machines. The manifest cause-and-effect sequence is deceptive, our mastery of it rings hollow. It takes a highly specialized expert to know how a TV or computer really works. Unfortunately, for our children and often their parents too, this incomprehensibility and necessary acceptance of it extend beyond complex machinery to all aspects of their experience. They tell us that orange juice comes from cans and cans come from the supermarket, what we do not need goes in the trash and then goes into the garbage truck. Things appear and disappear. Their comings and goings make no sense and there is no access to experiences that would explain them and prompt inquiries for deeper understanding. It has seemed to us that the work on understanding the life cycle in the context of familiar flowers and vegetables is so enthusiastically received because it provides opportunities really to understand and master daily experiences and motivates further learning because a base of knowledge that ''hangs together'' engenders hope and trust that more things will, with effort, make sense and bring a feeling of mastery. In this way, and only in this way, does learning make us feel good and adds to our self-esteem.

10

Learning to Enjoy Circle Time

ERNA FURMAN

Many, if not most, of us who work with under-fives in pre-schools, toddler groups, and daycare centers share a happy fantasy. We picture ourselves comfortably seated with book in hand, reading a lovely story to our charges who surround us in a nice semicircle. They squat on a cozy rug or sit nicely in their little chairs, their faces shining with pleasure and their eyes riveted on each picture page as they listen to our words, eagerly responding to our questions. At the end, they get up contentedly and go on to the next thing, almost thanking us as they tell us, or each other, how much they liked the book and how nice it will be to have story time again. In this lovely fantasy we feel so good about the happy time we shared with our pupils, and so good about laying the solid foundation for their future ability to enjoy and use books which will be so crucial to their later learning and pleasure in living.

Alas, like most happy fantasies, it contrasts sharply with the reality of circle time in our various preschool settings, the more so the younger the children and the fancier and more artistic the book. Even getting seated is a hassle, with Josh never ready in time, Jimmy unwilling to join us and preferring to play on his own, and Mary and Emily always intent on taking the same seat and shoving each other out of it. Margaret needs to sit next to us on one side and Jeremy on the other side to help them keep out of trouble, and this provokes cries of protest from others who also want to sit next to us. And in the meantime John and Ian, who definitely wanted to sit with one another, have begun to tickle and touch, and their neighbors raise complaints of "He's in my space!" We hurry to settle things down and promise them and ourselves that all will be well as soon as we get to reading our nice book. Things may indeed calm down for a little while, but not for long. One is sure to need to touch the book, another needs to look at it so closely as to almost hog it for himself, to the accompaniment of others' calls of "I can't see." John and Ian have resumed tickling each other and are now rolling on the floor. Margaret is not content to sit next to us and is trying to get onto our lap. Two or three youngsters are quietly absorbed sucking their thumbs or rubbing themselves and yawning, but their minds are not on us or the book. One needs to go to the bathroom. Jimmy, off in his corner, has started to bang things around and needs special help from our assistant. We try, more or less, to get through our story anyway, but our voice has become louder and a bit more tense, and the pages are turned faster. Some children speak up, but their comments are unrelated to the story or to our questions. Instead, they embrace a common underlying theme we might term, "Look at me!" The end is neither quietly contented nor appreciative. Leaving circle time can turn into running, pushing, and loud voices. And we, instead of feeling good, feel harassed, a bit angry at the children and at ourselves.

What went wrong? Are the children simply ill-behaved and beset by difficulties? Are they not ready for books because their parents have not read with them? Did we choose the wrong book, or did we not read it well enough to engage their interest? Sometimes there is a bit of truth in the answers to all these questions. Most of all, however, the trouble lies in that we tend not to appreciate all it takes to be able to enjoy a book the teacher reads to a group. It is really quite a complex achievement, and since our task as preschool educators is to help them get there, let us look at some of the many steps it involves.

READING WITH MOMMY

Books, like toys and activities, become meaningful when they are part of the very young child's one-to-one relationship with his primary caregiver, the mother or mothering person. Most mothers of our two- and three-year-old new entrants inform us that their youngsters love books. Observation of the mother-child couples in the Hanna Perkins Mother-Toddler Group readily confirms their claim (E. Furman, 1992, 1993). Some toddlers even choose books to read with Mommy at the very start of class; all of them eagerly turn to books later when they are a bit tired or in need of comfort, or just for a calm respite. It is a nice twosome time, a bit at a distance from the rest of us. There usually is a favorite book or two, which mother and child enjoy equally and which they are content to read over and over. The pleasure lies in the security of the familiar rather than in exploring the new. To the child, nestled in mother's arms, listening to her voice, perhaps sucking his thumb, the book is very much like a lullaby. Even when the toddler is more active, turning the pages, naming the items mother points to, or chiming in with her, the book is still at best an accompaniment to much gratifying mutual bodily contact and exclusive emotional closeness, and all bodily needs are immediately met as a part of it, be it wiping a runny nose, or interrupting to use the toilet, or still wetting into their pampers, as younger toddlers are apt to do during these cozy times.

In short, loving books with Mommy is a beginning, and a very good beginning, but it is a far cry from enjoying books read by a teacher in a group of peers. Many mothers know that. Even as they are sure their toddler loves books and that they will sit with him at circle time and tend to his needs and comforts, they shake their heads in worried anticipation and say, "I'm afraid he won't be able to manage circle time for the whole ten minutes. I may not even get him to come and sit down there with me." We agree that she may be right. Circle time is quite hard, but we shall prepare for it and work on it bit by bit with Mom's help. To start with, she and we will talk about circle time at snack, anticipating that after snack and cleanup each will sit with his or her Mommy in the special marked place on the rug, and we shall sing and do things with the teacher. It is a nice time, but one has to be a big toddler to have that fun, and so everyone will have to try hard and learn all the many things we have to do to act like big toddlers. The first thing is staying with Mommy in one's place and not playing with toys. Needless to say, most

toddlers want to get up as soon as they have sat down and rum-
mage on the shelves for a desired toy, so this is a very hard first
step. Mommy and teachers help by valuing and praising every
effort toward achieving it. Even though our initial circle times
may last only five minutes, the accomplishment of sitting through
it without playing with something is so great that it deserves
special recognition. It is followed by many more steps in mastery
and self-control. Each is singled out as a hard but worthwhile
goal to work toward together, and with each the back-and-forth
process of getting there is the focus of support, with many opportunities to learn to feel good about oneself. Circle time does get
to be more and more fun along the way, but the most important
part is the learning of all the skills it entails.

FROM MOTHER TO TEACHER

Some of the necessary developmental steps are primarily in the
teachers' minds. We share them with the mothers but not explicitly with the children. The most obvious one is the crucial step
of learning to relate with the teacher as teacher. This, like all the
other steps, can be embarked on during the toddler phase, but it
remains an ongoing task throughout the preschool years, with
true achievement extending into early elementary school. The
teacher-pupil relationship is quite different from the relationship
with mother or mother substitutes, be they family members or
professional caregivers. It is a relationship that excludes bodily
contact as well as most need fulfilling interactions, and focuses
on learning together about activities that do not provide bodily
or impulse gratifications. We do not kiss and cuddle with our
pupils; we help them to feed, dress, and toilet themselves, rather
than doing it for them. We do not tend to them when they are
ill, do not spend nights with them or share vacations. The teacher-
pupil relationship is always time-limited, covering certain hours
of certain days for, at best, a certain number of years. That all
takes a long time to understand and accept. The younger the
child, the more readily does he view us as a potential mother
substitute. In daycare centers we actually also are mother substitutes, but in nursery schools we are not, and during circle times
we are always very much the teacher.

Helping youngsters to build a teacher-pupil relationship to enjoy interests and learning activities is an ongoing part of the whole curriculum, but circle time puts it especially into focus. Since we cannot do "mommy things" with them during this period, it is a big help to have mother participate. She provides the cuddling and holding as the young toddler still sits on her lap, cradles between her legs, or leans against her. She can also tend to his needs which he cannot yet meet himself, be it nose wiping or toileting, and she can assist him with impulse control which he is also just learning to do for himself, be it keeping his legs from kicking (or kicking others) or keeping his shirt on instead of exposing his tummy. Not least, her pleasurable participation in the circle time activities helps him to enjoy them and fosters the shared relationship with the teacher. No wonder the toddlers and young preschoolers have such a hard time at circle without their mothers! They miss Mom and her comforts and ministrations, and they cannot use us to provide them at circle time because that is when we are busy doing our teacher thing for everyone. And that, of course, is one of the hardest-to-learn parts of the teacher-pupil relationship, namely, that teachers have to be shared. It is a difficult lesson to learn during any period of the school or center day, but it is especially hard during circle time because there is minimal, if any, one-to-one interaction. No wonder the children do their best to insist on getting exclusive attention by calling out, crawling into the middle of the circle, hogging the space in front of the teacher and her book, or creating a disturbance. Worst off are some of the "good" children who just give up, withdraw into themselves and/or comfort themselves with their bodies—sucking their thumbs, wiggling, twirling their hair, masturbating.

Until the relationship with the teacher is more meaningful and all the body needs and urges are more in the child's control, it is therefore a big help to him, and to the teacher, to have mother with him. In daycare centers and preschools it helps when mother can participate during circle time at least for a few days. Even one day is better than none. When she knows all it takes, then she, her child, and the teacher can continue to build on the memory of her presence and include her in shared talks about work and progress on circle time skills. She, as it were, remains at circle time mentally, even if not in body. This also helps her

and us not to forget that circle time, because of its many demands
on the child's personality, is a prime Mommy-missing time. After
all, even as grownups, we still tend to recreate the early intimacy
of reading books with Mommy, when we like to curl up with a
book, in bed or in an armchair, feeling cozy.

However, that does not mean that reading books with
Mommy always remains the most favored or most appropriate
interaction. As toddlers master the circle time skills and their
relationship with us intensifies, they spontaneously pull away
from Mom, want to sit a bit apart from her, protest her attempts
at intimacy, and pay little heed to whether she participates or
just sits there quietly. Much later, being read to by Mommy can
prove a source of conflict and resentment when the older child
wants to begin to read rather than be read to, or when her fluency
makes him feel inferior. Indeed, in time, learning with a teacher
becomes preferable to learning with mother. But this can only
come about when we put much thought and effort into helping
the very young to learn about a teacher-pupil relationship and
assist them with the transition from reading books with Mommy
to participating at circle time.

One of the ways we maximize our contact with the children
during circle time is by addressing them directly, avoiding intermediaries. Let me explain what I mean. We all know that any
lecture is much more enjoyable for the audience (and much more
appreciated) when the speaker talks rather than reads. The printed
page, even when it is the speaker's own text, gets in the way of
the relationship with the listener. It is an intermediary. This is
even more true with texts that are not the speaker's own. Since
most of the children's books we use are not authored by ourselves, they inevitably speak with someone else's voice, using
the author's ideas and words, not ours. The same holds for tapes,
films, records. They introduce a third party, an outsider at that,
into the teacher-pupil twosome and, by doing so, interfere with it.
Sometimes teachers use such intermediaries to give themselves a
break, or to engage the children's attention. With young children
this is not helpful because our goal is to use our relationship to
help them remain focused on us and to resist diversions. It is
more helpful to have a short circle time, which does not exceed
their or our limits, than to extend it with the use of tapes, records,
films, or even books. As we shall discuss later, enjoying and

using books is a special, rather advanced developmental step. Therefore much has to be accomplished before our youngsters are ready for books at circle time. In the meantime, it works best to start with short little stories, songs, and rhymes, all told, sung, and acted out by and with the teacher. This way we look at and listen to each other most directly.

TAKING CARE OF ONE'S NEEDS AND WANTS

Young children are still at the mercy of their bodily needs which have to be met right away and which, much of the time, still require assistance from a caring adult. When they are hungry, they need food now; when they have to use the toilet, they need to do so now; when they are tired, they need to rest now, otherwise their functioning deteriorates quickly into uncontrolled behavior or withdrawal. Likewise, their impulses press for immediate discharge and it takes help from the caring adult to put on the brake. When they are angry, pushing and shoving, kicking and throwing things, come naturally, especially when the adult's attention is not fully and helpfully available. Excitement too bursts forth at the drop of a hat, may show in chasing and wrestling with others, in exposing himself or peeking, or in wiggling and touching himself. As parents and educators, much of our time is spent on helping children to recognize and care for their own needs, and on restraining and modifying their impulses. It is a slow process. When we talked about reading books with Mommy, we noted just how much the mother's close availability satisfies the child's needs and wants and, at the same time, contains them and guards against excess. We also noted how sitting with mother at circle time serves to fulfill this role while, at the same time, mother's participation serves as a bridge to joining in activities with the teacher. When we ask our little ones to be at circle time without their mothers, and even without our one-to-one mothering attention, we may ask too much self-control of them.

How can we improve the situation? In the overall curriculum we help most by supporting and valuing our charges' progress toward self-care, i.e., taking care of their own bodily needs, and their progress toward self-control of impulses. At circle time, we help by spelling out each of the requirements, sometimes on an individual basis, and, as with the first achievement of sitting down and not getting up to play with toys, we prepare and enlist the child's effort by encouragement and praise. If Molly works hard at keeping her feet to her own space, and if Jimmy and Ian agree to sit separately because it helps them not to touch each other, those are worthy goals for circle time, deserving of pride in oneself, of the teacher's admiration, and of a special good report to Mom at pickup time.

We can also help by making circle time short and by scheduling it when the children's needs are more or less quiescent, and their impulse control is optimal because they are not yet too tired and have not been stimulated by energetic activity; for example, circle time fits in quite well in the morning after the snack/bathrooming/cleanup period and before large muscle play. This timing contrasts with that of many schools and centers who use circle time as a calming-down period, either after outdoor play or before rest time. This may work well for some of the older preschoolers who are already pretty much in charge of their needs and impulses and can use the teacher primarily as a teacher, but it does not work well for the developmentally younger ones who are still in the process of acquiring these masteries and for whom circle time is still a hard challenge.

Another way we can help is by structuring circle time so as to provide opportunities for legitimate discharge of minor bodily tensions. What I have in mind is the many songs and rhymes in which the children participate actively with their voices, with hand movements, with shakers, or with body movements. These have to be carefully gauged so as not to become too stimulating; for example, the hand movements of the familiar ''Open, shut them'' rhyme usually serve well as discharge, whereas ''Ring-around-the-rosey'' can become too much unless carefully prepared for and monitored (we sit down, rather than fall down, at the end!). Sitting quietly and passively is especially hard—another reason for postponing the use of books—whereas doing along with the teacher allows for constructive activity.

In addition to learning to take care of his wants and needs, the young child has to accomplish another developmental step in order to enjoy circle time. He has to learn that pleasure and satisfaction can be derived from interests and activities that provide no direct or immediate bodily gratification. Singing songs, cutting out pictures, throwing and catching a ball, in fact all the things we help our pupils learn to like and feel good about, are such new tastes for them. We know how difficult a step it is when we watch their painting deteriorate into messing, their block building turn into boisterous crashing, their scissors deviate from the paper to attack the table or even the child who sits next to them. How often we have to intervene, to admonish, to redirect, to stop! How much we have to use our own enjoyment of nonbodily pursuits to enlist and support their efforts and achievements in this area and to divert them from the tempting familiar bodily ones: ''But Jamie, you started on such a beautiful painting and now it's turning into such a big puddle with the paint running over the edges. I don't think you'll end up feeling proud of it and wanting to take it home. So how about wiping your brush well and doing your good job. Do you think you can fix it, or would it be better to start over again with a new paper?'' Sometimes we offer the lure of doing things and feeling good like a big boy or girl, in contrast to the messing which is the only thing littler kids can have fun with. In fact, the whole teacher-pupil relationship rests on sharing and learning about these new nonbodily pleasures. We hope that the more the child masters his needs and impulses, the more energy will be available for him to join us in developing the new pleasures. Circle time consists of these new pleasures. To learn to enjoy them requires mastery of the earlier bodily pleasures and a good enough teacher-pupil relationship, so that our enjoyment of the new pleasures will entice the child to join us in learning and experiencing them for himself. It happens slowly, but each attempt is worth encouraging and admiring.

A teacher's own enjoyment is an important prerequisite. If we do not really have fun with all the little songs and rhymes, and later pictures and books, the children will sense it. It will become a boring or grim chore, not the gateway to new horizons. But beware when the teacher gets drawn into the old fun instead of conveying the new! Some parents and educators think that the best way to get the children really involved in stories (or any other new experience, for that matter) is to make them as sensational and exciting as possible. This can be achieved through the content of what we present (many cartoons specialize in this, but so do some rhymes, stories, and books) or through the way we act it out—a boisterous ring-around-the-rosey is a mild example. The educator's intent may be good and the children's participation is assured, but the fun is far from what we want to lead them toward and nothing will have been learned, except perhaps that the grownups really only like just what the little ones like and cannot be relied upon to help with self-control. The aftermath of these flings shows not only in the difficult transition to the next activity, but may linger and invade functioning in other areas. Cause and effect are often hard to trace in children's behavior. They may loudly proclaim and show how much they "love" the stimulating excitement of such circle times, just as they "love" and seek out similarly stimulating TV programs or roughhousing. Neither they nor we may readily link this fun to the later rambunctiousness, irritability, difficulty with concentration, messing at meals, or a host of other troubles that look like naughtiness out of the blue.

FROM TEACHER TO BOOK

The ultimate goal of introducing children to books is that they will be able to enjoy books and use them to learn from by relating to what an unknown, absent author presents in them. The achievement of this goal lies well in the future for our youngsters and is often never achieved, even by adults. Hence the need of so many people to meet the author, to find out about his or her personal life, to get into a direct relationship. Some people can only read and enjoy a book when they have made such a contact and some, even then, find the personal contact with the author more satisfying than his book. Yet being able to enjoy and use books is, in our society, not only a pleasure but a necessity in training for and maintaining a job. So we want to do our best to give our young ones a good start. Beyond reading books with Mommy, it is the teacher-pupil relationship that provides the next important step. And its focus is circle time.

When our youngsters are far enough along in their masteries to manage circle time with songs and rhymes and movements, we can start by devoting a small fraction of the period to showing them pictures—just one or two at first, perhaps three, even four later. Big pictures can be seen by the whole group without having to be passed around, and they can be lined up next to each other against a board facing the semicircle, so that every child can look at all of them. Nobody needs to worry that ''I can't see'' or ''He always gets to see it first.'' Pictures introduce the new lesson of looking only with our eyes, i.e., not touching with our hands, and looking only from our place, i.e., not coming up close—difficult achievements, each the focus of special effort, support, and praise. It helps a lot when the same pictures are used on a few successive occasions, and when they are displayed on a wall or board between circle times, so that each child has a chance also to touch them, to come up close, and to have them to himself when it is not circle time.

What kind of pictures should we choose? It is so difficult for little children to transfer their perception and knowledge of real things to their pictorial representation that the beginning pictures should be selected to show the simplest and most familiar items, such as a favorite food, a boy or a girl, a car, dog, cat. We then graduate to pictures of simple, familiar activities, such as a child sleeping, eating, dressing, or a Mommy walking with her child or feeding their dog. What we choose, and in which order, will not only depend on the complexity, but on the children's individual experiences, always ranging from the more to the less familiar. The important point is that for quite some time children can only relate to a picture when they can recognize their own familiar experience in it. In time they will be ready for some of the pictures to show something new (but not too new). We usually choose the something new that one or more children have talked about having encountered. For example, when we looked at a few pictures of local animals, a couple of children told of having seen a raccoon in their yard. So we added a raccoon picture. Sometimes we choose the something new as part of a series. For example, when we looked at a few pictures of children engaged in familiar activities, we added a picture of the less familiar activity of children petting a lamb. Pictures also pick up on interests and activities that are part of the overall curriculum. For example, in toddler group, putting on mittens is an important theme and includes tracing hands and cutting out paper mittens, singing our mitten activity rhyme, putting mittens on our flannel board paper person, and perhaps showing some pictures of children dressed for the cold outdoors with mittens.

Books come in when pictures are mastered. Even the simplest book usually has more than four pages and therefore exceeds the picture series. Also, pictures on book pages can only be looked at one at a time. The first books consist of simple sequences of familiar items, page by page, like the earlier pictures. Then come the more coherent sequences, again focused on the young child's own daily experiences, such as the *I Can Do It By Myself* book (Goldsborough, 1981) which depicts a child's areas of self-care, or *The Very Little Dog* (Skaar, cca 1950) which shows a puppy growing into a big dog, cashing in on each child's impatient wish to grow big. Some books are very close to the young child's emotional experience but in a frightening way, and therefore not helpful, for example, the well-known *Are You My Mother* (Eastman, 1960). How scary to think one would forget who one's mother was!

Sometimes children's books with very suitable contents become incomprehensible because the illustrations are so elaborately or abstractly artistic that children find it hard to recognize in them the reality they know. The illustrations have to be as clearly related to the child's perception as the content. It takes a long time before the children are ready for books that introduce new ideas or experiences and new ways of depicting them. Even then it helps when we relate them to ongoing class interests and activities. *The Carrot Seed* (Krauss, 1945), for example, is quite an advanced book. We combine it with our many gardening activities during the latter part of the school year. Last of all come books that deal with fantasy and imaginary contents. These can usually begin to be understood and enjoyed by older preschoolers.

As we take our young children through the painstaking, slow process of learning to enjoy and use books, and as we enjoy with them each little step along the way, we enable them to make the shared pleasure and achievement a part of themselves. It will not only remain a fond memory, but will form the foundation for using books on their own. Just as reading books with Mommy became a bridge to reading books with the teacher, so the relationship with the teacher will become a bridge to new teachers in elementary school, and even a bridge to relating to books by unknown, absent authors.

Returning to the happy fantasy of the lovely circle time which I described at the start, I fear it is like with Moses and the promised land—a thrilling glimpse into a future so distant that we shall have little chance of ever getting there. In the meantime, our pleasure and satisfaction have to come from helping our youngsters find their laborious way toward it. Getting there can be at least half the fun.

11

Where, When, and How to Go on Field Trips

YVETTE ANNE HOFFMAN
in collaboration with CAROL EBER, ERNA
FURMAN, KATE O'ROURKE, NANCY SABATH,
and BARBARA WELCH

Every teacher in a preschool or daycare program is asked the same questions from new and old parents regarding field trips—where do you go, how often do you go away from school, how do you get there? Many factors are involved in planning good field trip experiences for young children. Parent input is essential in this planning. Occasionally, however, parents' enthusiasm for doing something they enjoy interferes with their understanding of young children. Contrary to what many parents feel must be a boring experience to "just play at nursery school," a young child finds security in a familiar place, in repetition, in a definite schedule, and will be better able to learn one new thing in the same surroundings than to assimilate many new things in a strange place.

During the first two months of preschool, children are busy adjusting to their new surroundings, new teacher, peers and routine, and to separation from Mommy. They are not ready to take an extended trip away from school, but may be able to extend their knowledge by visiting its immediate surroundings. The

The contents of this chapter were formulated during discussions of the Cleveland Center for Research in Child Development Consultation Group by its participants and with Erna Furman as consultant.

147

teacher knows her group best and can judge when they are ready to take their first trip—for example, a tour of the building that houses their school or center. This may include a visit to the director's office to see her desk, a view behind the door that leads to the attic, where the teacher keeps the napkins, cups, paper towels, and other school supplies, and then a walk downstairs to visit the other offices in the building to see the people working at the typewriters, answering telephones, and working at computers. Such a trip could include a visit to the basement to find the furnace that heats the school like the one in "Mike Mulligan." The man who changes the smoke alarm batteries and light bulbs is another important stop on this trip. The last stop may be the school gym that is used in winter by the children so that its size and location can be compared to the classrooms. The trip may later be extended to revisit the school playground they visited with Mommy in the spring, before they came to school, and reinforce their understanding that Mommy knows where to pick them up when school is over if they go outside to play.

The next step in planning for field trips is to select places the children are likely to have visited with their parents. This gives them an opportunity to experience the familiar place with a new set of rules, to develop self-reliance, and perhaps to include some new items and perspective. Hence, the teacher chooses not new things, but familiar places of interest in the community. She needs to explore the community and find out what children could assimilate through visits and what would contribute to their education. Again, the amount of familiarity is a major factor in the selection process.

In choosing trips, consideration should also be given to the group of children involved, what may be good for one group this year may not be good for a different group next year. Whatever the chosen trip, it should not take longer than one-half to three-quarter hours, and there must always be preparation before the trip begins. The children's abilities and attention span make it unhelpful to plan longer visits.

RECOMMENDED TRIPS

1. Story hour for the class, only at the local library.
2. Supermarket—at a slow time if possible. What an excellent chance for the teacher to go through the store with

the children and point out the fruits and vegetables that look alike and those that are different in texture, find out how many things are orange or red, or the number of different kinds of potatoes. There are endless possibilities for sequencing, discrimination, etc., in the produce department as well as in the aisles of canned foods! Different sizes and shapes of boxes and containers can be found. Then, just before returning to school, the children can buy their own can of juice for snack time with their own money.

3. A walk to the local mailbox or post office to mail a Valentine or Mother's Day card.

4. A trip to the paint store for sample chips of related colors that can be used for experiments with colors or collage work at school.

5. The local park to observe signs of spring and test our senses—the wildflowers, migrating birds that are seen through binoculars made out of tissue tubes and heard calling through the trees, smelling wild wintergreen that smells just like gum, and touching the bark on the trees. Each season offers its own specialties!

6. A new building that is under construction followed by weekly visits by the foreman of construction so that he can explain what is happening to the building. Many foreman are delighted to participate!

Repeated field trips to the same location are especially rewarding. Far from being boring, they afford youngsters opportunities for mastery and increased learning. They helpfully combine the pleasurable recognition of the familiar with the stimulation of the new as the children are often better able to observe and integrate details and changes within an already known framework. One of the most successful field trips was undertaken by a preschool that visited their almost adjacent empty lot every month throughout the year, noting the many seasonal and other changes as well as discovering previously overlooked items.

Often trips that are planned to go outside of the community to unfamiliar places and to involve more than a few minutes of driving may not be suitable for nursery groups at all. If these trips are attempted, they should be scheduled toward the very end of the school year and limited to one. These may include selected areas of the zoo and of museums, or a small farm with just a few animals. Such trips are best reserved for the kindergarten youngsters for whom they are more appropriate.

The teacher/director as a professional educator can best recognize the needs and interests of the children involved and should have the final authority on the selection, number of trips and where, when and how to go on trips. As the parents have entrusted the school or center to care for their children, it is important that the teacher/director take time to explain to them, at a meeting or through a monthly newsletter, the school's philosophy on trips and what is educationally most helpful to and enjoyed by the children.

PREPARATION

Preliminary visits to the proposed sites are necessary. The teacher needs to get to know the details of the site and the people involved in the visit with whom she also has to discuss the school's philosophy and requirements.

Preparation of the children comes next. Each trip requires the same approach. The more knowledge the children have about leaving school on a trip and returning safely, the more comfortable they are about it, and the more able to learn from it. For example, the children can help plan their walk to the mail box to mail the Valentines they made for Mommy and Daddy. Two weeks prior to their walk, the children can construct and paint their own mail box after observing the one on their way to and from school. Dramatic play can include a postman delivering letters the other children have written. He can place them into their mail boxes in school. During music time, the children can play a version of ''Duck, duck, goose'' that has a postman dropping a letter behind someone's back. For story time, the teacher can either read or show the filmstrip ''A Letter to Amy.'' While the children are in circle time, the teacher can write a picture story with the children about what they will see on the way, how far they will walk, who will help them cross the street, who will pick up the mail from the box, where it goes, and how it is delivered to their house. Also at this time, the questions and concerns, such as, "Can I still see our school from the mail box?" or "Will Mommy know where to pick me up outside of school?" can be answered. After the trip, the children can draw a picture of their impressions of their walk, and dictate a story to the teacher that can be placed in their very own copy of their story books to be shared with family and friends later. While recalling the trip during the next days, the teacher can relieve any anxiety caused by observing the unexpected—and there always is at least one unexpected—such as a dead squirrel along the curb. Field trips taken mid-week allow for preparation and followup.

PRACTICAL ARRANGEMENTS FOR THE TRIP

1. A meeting with parents at the beginning of the school year to discuss the whole topic of trips, policy on leaving the building, school insurance, and seat belts.
2. Field trip permission slips. These should designate the trip, date and time, and be filled out and signed by the parents prior to each trip. A reminder with all pertinent information about the trip can be placed in the monthly newsletter sent out by the teacher. At this time, a parent should have the option of allowing their child to participate in that trip.
3. Distance. Field trips should be planned within a ten-minute driving radius of school to the designated site. This is for safety reasons as well as to keep the children from becoming restless through sitting in the car too long.
4. Safety requirements. Every child is required to be in a seat belt or car seat by state law, and in an insured car.
5. Car drivers. In keeping with the school's insurance policy, the teachers may need to accompany the mother driver in her car and may not be allowed to drive themselves. The school's insurance policy should be investigated. Also, teachers need to choose parent drivers not merely for their willingness, but primarily for their ability to drive safely.
6. Adult supervision. A safe ratio of adults to children has to be considered carefully along with the type of trip

and the teacher's tested judgment of being able to keep
them safe.

7. Mother helpers on the trip must leave younger siblings
   at home.
8. Whenever possible, appoint a field trip chairman who
   should arrange the number of cars needed for transportation and/or the number of mother helpers, a snack if
   needed (such as a picnic in the park), and any other
   details as they arise, to help the teacher.
9. Frequency of trips depends on facilities available, the
   nature of the children, and the time needed to absorb
   the previous trip and to prepare for the next one.
10. Visits to the proposed sites are necessary. The teacher
    needs to get to know the site and the people involved
    in the visit so that the school's philosophy and require-
    ments are known to all.

Successful field trips can be achieved if we keep in mind
the basic guideline of visiting the most familiar place first, pro-
ceeding to the less familiar, then to the least familiar.

PART III

12

Children in Hospitals—As Patients and as Visitors

ERNA FURMAN

Since the mid-seventies, the Cleveland Center for Research in Child Development has given a course for child life workers. Their purpose is to help hospitalized children and their families with the emotional stresses engendered by illness, by medical and surgical treatment, and by separation from home. At first one might think that children in hospitals are far removed from children in preschools and that we who work with physically healthy children would have little in common with those who work with seriously ill children. However, the very difficult, often tragic situations that child life workers need to cope with and the puzzlements that confront them concern the very children who were in ordinary families and preschools before they became ill and who, it is hoped, will return to them. The ill children's responses have to be assessed and understood within the framework of their phase-appropriate personality development in order to find ways of assisting them and their families with mastery.

I shall not present shocking examples of the many painful cases that come up for discussion. However, I shall discuss some areas in which child life workers and preschool educators have cooperated with benefit to each other and to the children and families in their care.

CHILDREN AS PATIENTS

The First area concerns preschool pupils who become hospital patients. It happens unfortunately all too often that a young child

155

requires hospitalization, either for treatment of a chronic disease or of a sudden emergency. The preschool educator who maintains a good working relationship with the parents is usually one of the first to hear about it, at a time when the family dreads stepping into the strange and stressful world of the hospital where many people they do not know will do to their child things they do not always understand. It is of great help to parents and child then if the teacher or caregiver can tell them about the child life worker's role, can sometimes even give them the name of a specific child life worker to turn to, and can assure them that this person will be available to answer questions, to prepare for procedures, to assist with concerns, and to help make the hospital stay as comfortable as possible. When the child life worker is, in this way, introduced by the educator the family trusts, he or she has a much better chance at building a relationship with them. With planned hospitalizations, it is even possible and helpful for the parents and child to meet with the child life worker before the scheduled admission and to feel better prepared for it.

The child life worker, in turn, can help the nursery school teacher at the time of the child's discharge and when he is ready to return to his school or daycare center. With the child life worker's help, the parents will know better, and be able to share, what was especially stressful for the child, to what extent he could be helped to master it, what still might concern him and need further support. In some instances parents have also given permission for direct contact, such as by telephone, between child life worker and teacher. It is often hard for the teacher to know what difficulties may manifest themselves after a hospitalization, what the child might say about his experiences to the other children, how to help him and his peers understand what happened, perhaps even how to explain visible aftereffects of treatment. When one pupil goes to the hospital, all his classmates are affected and need assistance in coping with the threat and the questions this poses for them. The parents and children who have benefited from a child life worker's help will often be more knowledgeable about these matters and helpful to the teacher in her task. They are also likely to have achieved better mastery of their stress so that it interferes less in their subsequent readjustment.

Over the years we have had experience with quite a number of cases in which such cooperation between teacher and child life worker proved worthwhile for all. Among these was a girl with leukemia who required repeated hospitalizations and whose physical appearance was affected by the treatments she received; one boy underwent surgery to correct an undescended testicle; another boy had an emergency hospitalization for pneumonia; a girl was casted following an operation for a minor foot deformity, and another was casted for a bone fracture.

Sometimes parents have approached the teacher not about their preschooler, but about a younger or older sibling's hospitalization. There again a referral to the child life worker was greatly appreciated. The teacher benefited from the closer relationship her help to the family fostered, as well as from knowing better the life circumstances that currently affected the preschooler in her charge and being able to help him.

I am not suggesting that the teacher be privy to all details of a child's health troubles or that she should take over the parents' role of helping their child with his illness and its care. Least of all do I imply that the teacher share with all the classmates and their families her knowledge of one child's medical problems and hospital experiences. Illness is a person's private affair and needs to be respected as such. With the peers, it is as unhelpful to give no explanation as it is to overwhelm the youngsters with all the details, especially as these can be frightening. At the same time it is important for the teacher to be able to address simply, sensibly, and sympathetically the concerns that the ill child brings into the school setting and their inevitable effect on the other children.

Many hospitals now have a child life service. In the Cleveland area, our Center and School have served as an intermediary. Local educators and caregivers are usually already familiar with the role of child life work and, when in need, contact us for the name of a child life worker who has worked with us and to whom parents can turn for assistance. An intermediary is not essential, however. Teachers can, on their own, inquire about the availability of a child life service at their local hospitals and alert parents to it when the occasion arises. A satisfactory hospital experience by one child and family becomes the basis for knowing individual child life workers and relying on them for future referrals and advice. Educators can also contact child life workers and learn about their service before an ill child needs them. Such "preventive" cooperation between the adult professionals is helpful.

THE DRAWBACKS OF EDUCATIONAL TRIPS TO HOSPITALS

"Preventive" educational contacts are, however, not helpful when they involve the children. Many hospitals conduct "tours" for nursery school classes. Many preschool centers take their youngsters on such visits as one of their field trips. The intent is good—to acquaint children with the health facilities in their community, to help them learn about hospitals while they are healthy, and to develop trust in hospital care in case they need it at a later point. Unfortunately, it does not work out that way.

Child life workers found that the children were often so frightened and overwhelmed by what they were exposed to that they could not seem to learn from it or gain reassurance. At first an attempt was made to select and structure better what would be shown and told. No matter how hard the child life workers tried, however, something always happened that was not part of the planned tour. Instead of focusing on all the attractive toys in the hospital playroom, the children's eyes remained riveted on a little patient with leg casts, in a wheelchair. Just walking along the corridor, the children saw revealed through half-open doors emaciated or bandaged youngsters or beds surrounded by strange apparatus. Even from behind closed doors occasional moans, cries, or protests could be heard. These perceptions, usually unheeded by the accompanying adults, proved invariably more impressive than the scheduled items.

In truth, it is impossible to enter a hospital without experiencing encounters with illness and equipment that shock and bewilder the unaccustomed adult. The impact on young children is all the greater, beyond their scope of intellectual and emotional mastery, even if an attempt were made to explain it all. Since, however, the preschoolers sense that they are not meant to notice these incidental experiences, they often do not refer to them or question them and are condemned to keep the resulting inner turmoil a guilty secret.

These repeated observations convinced the child life workers in our course that young children's groups should not tour the hospital, and they set about achieving this goal in cooperation with the other responsible staff and volunteers. At most of our regional hospitals there have been no educational trips for preschoolers for several years. Some preschool educators made similar observations during and after these trips and have taken hospital tours off their centers' list of field trips. However, there are still many hospitals that welcome preschool groups, and many nursery schools who consider these trips educational, unaware of their undesirable emotional impact.

These considerations apply equally to class visits to nursing homes, often intended to afford children an opportunity to bring pleasure to the elderly sick. Unfortunately, there are no child life workers in these settings to alert teachers and parents to the inherent difficulties, but they do exist. The mere physical and often mental debilitation of the nursing home residents is shocking to young children and untempered by the bonds of individual relationships, such as might be available with one's loved grandparent. Fear and even disgust tend to override the benefits of doing a kindness and, as a result, leave the youngster not only upset, but also guilty.

CHILDREN AS VISITORS

Preschoolers' group visits in hospitals are likewise contraindicated when the aim is to visit an ill classmate. On these occasions, too, it is impossible to get to the particular child's room without encountering disturbing unscheduled sights and sounds. The impact is further intensified when signs of the patient's illness or treatments are witnessed, even if he or she is "on the mend." Young children feel much safer when a peer's illness is thoughtfully discussed in the familiar setting of their own classroom and when contact is maintained indirectly, by means of sending cards, pictures, tapes, or gifts. We know how hard it often is for preschoolers to differentiate their own from others' upsets, how often we help them by reminding them that another's sadness, anger, or uncontrolled behavior is "his trouble" and does not have to be theirs. Similarly with illness, a child's helpful line between self and other is better maintained and leaves more room for appropriate sympathy when he or she is not confronted with the ill peer in the stressful immediacy of the hospital room.

Although there is a big difference between a class visit and an individual child's visit to the hospital or nursing home with his Mom or Dad, some of the caveats apply. They apply especially if such a visit is meant to please the ill person without considering the experience from the child's point of view, or if it is intended to be a substitute for verbal explanation about the illness. Sometimes parents are so shocked and upset themselves about the illness of a relative, friend, or of their own other child, especially a newborn, that they find it difficult to clarify the situation with their preschooler in words, and hope that seeing will be believing. However, the sights and sounds the young child perceives during such visits lead to confusion and misunderstanding and result in the child becoming even more shocked than his parents. Child life workers often report their concern about these youngsters who may even be found wandering around crying or bewildered, while their parents are tending to the patient or talking with the nurse or doctor.

Yet there are situations in which young children can and should visit the hospital or nursing home with their mother or father, namely, when the personal contact is an attempt to support the emotional ties between the child and his loved one. This presupposes that the parent and child have discussed the nature of the illness and been in feeling touch with one another about it, and it applies especially to visiting someone with whom the child has maintained a very close important relationship. Most often this is the case with a hospitalized parent, sometimes also with a sibling or a grandparent in a nursing home. These reunions are often crucial to the child in mastering the stress of separation and concern over the loved one's health.

One hopes that, with the help of the in-tune well parent, the benefits will outweigh the worries engendered by the stressful observations. Even with this kind of individual hospital visit, however, parents need to appreciate the risks and be prepared to help the child cope with them. Children should visit only those ill family members who are conscious and able to be emotionally in touch with the child. Also, care need be taken to avoid or interrupt visits when the patient is undergoing procedures of a private, frightening, or disfiguring nature. The accompanying parent can prepare the child for possible scary or puzzling sights, can be alert to everything the child encounters in the hospital and sympathetic to the child's feelings about it. In doing so, he or she will find the right moments and ways of offering explanations and reassurance.

Having to shoulder their own and their child's upsets is a difficult task for parents. As they deliberate whether or not to take their child on such a hospital or nursing home visit and how to make it least stressful for him, they often turn for advice to the person they trust to know, i.e., their child's teacher. She can be very helpful to parent and child when she understands what is involved.

13

Sexual Abuse: Experiences with Prevention, Detection, and Treatment

ERNA FURMAN

WHAT IS SEXUAL ABUSE?

The term "sexual abuse" is widely used but rarely specifically defined or described. According to the dictionary, abuse connotes misuse and is described as "unreasonable or improper use or treatment" (Britannica, 1964). Sexual abuse of children, though not listed as such, refers to the sexual misuse, i.e., unreasonable and improper treatment, of a minor. This phrase covers the legal and psychological definitions, but it does not address their considerable differences. The law, reflecting current and local mores, varies from state to state, country to country, and often undergoes revisions. In any place, at any given time, it usually specifies certain practices, age range of abuser and abused and, in addition, lists those obligated to report on knowledge of sexual abuse to official agencies and under certain circumstances. Since teachers and caregivers are usually mandated to report, they need to be familiar with the law in their area, a task nowadays often accomplished with the help of required attendance of certified courses on recognition and reporting of sexual abuse. These legal obligations place a heavy burden on educators—and I shall address some aspects of it later—but they do not help them gauge and understand the emotional issues of sexual abuse, how and why they affect the child, the parents, and the involved professionals, or the fact that the child may experience abuse in situations that encompass a much wider range than those delineated by the law. To answer some of these questions we need to consider a psychological definition of child sexual abuse.

From a psychological point of view, all sexual matters, and sexual abuse particularly, are characterized by the feelings and impulses they involve, consciously and/or unconsciously, and by the way the personality copes with them. Sexual impulses, with their sensations and feelings of excitement, are part of our endowment, as is their intensification in response to stimulation. Stimulation may be mental, related to what we see, hear, or think, or it may be bodily. With adults, the most intense excitement is usually evoked through stimulation of the genitals, which also serve as the vehicle of discharge, while other forms and areas of stimulation play a lesser part. With children—and the more so, the younger they are—the genitals do not yet serve this primary function. Instead, excitement is generated and experienced in all bodily openings, through skin contact (such as rubbing, hugging, tickling, roughhousing), through active and passive kinesthetic sensations (such as energetic motor activity or being swung or rocked). Insofar as the personality has means of absorbing the excitement, it may be experienced as pleasurable. When the amount of excitement exceeds the available means—when the child is "overstimulated"—the personality has to resort to special measures of coping and discharging. This manifests itself not only in symptomatic behavior, but also interferes with progressive personality development. When the excitement is so intense that it altogether overwhelms the personality, leaving it shattered and deprived of all coping mechanisms, the child has been traumatized. His or her personality functioning and chances of growth have been disrupted in a major way.

Due to the immaturity of their coping mechanisms and avenues of discharge, infants and toddlers are most easily overstimulated and traumatized by the least forceful invasive types of stimulation, some of which may not be listed as illegal. Thus, from the child's point of view, and psychologically speaking, the nature and severity of sexual abuse needs to be gauged by its effect on the child's personality. As a result, and as we shall discuss later, detection of sexual abuse in young children often proceeds not merely by what the child tells us or even by bodily signs of injury or infection, but by tracing and understanding its effects on the child's behavior and overall personality growth. Whereas the law focuses only on the doer and his or her acts, the educator needs to consider the child's experience and its effects on functioning.

However, the abuser and what he or she does are not irrelevant to the child's experience and our efforts at understanding it. The effect of a sexual abuse will vary greatly with the role the abuser plays in the child's life; for example, whether he or she is a primary caregiver or a person with whom the child maintains a relationship (sibling, relative, family friend), or one to whom the parents have relegated the child's care (sitter, parent substitute), or a stranger. It will depend also on the age and sex of the abuser. What the abuser does is equally important. Its effect will vary greatly with the frequency of abuse, its suddenness, forcefulness, and bodily invasiveness, or gentle seductive approach enlisting the child's willing participation.

Not least, the impact on the child will be affected by the abuser's mental state. The child can sense, feel, and perceive the abuser's sexual and/or aggressive excitement, the urgency to gratify these impulses, and the extent to which this allows the abuser to consider the child as a person. Sexual abuse, both in the sense of "misuse" and of "unreasonable or improper use or treatment" implies self-gratification at the cost of consideration for the victim. This holds true for the tickler who cannot heed the pleas of the tickled child as well as for the perpetrator of forced perverse penetrations, but they span a wide range of relative lack of respect for the bodily and emotional integrity of the abused as a person. Total disregard is annihilating, and devastating in its effects. The degree to which the needs and rights of the child's self are ignored, overwhelmed, or destroyed plays a major part in the impact and effects of abuse. This needs to be taken into account.

LEARNING ABOUT SEXUAL ABUSE

At our Center and School, child analysts treat sexually abused children individually and intensively, devoting several years to

the work with each patient and family. This provides an unusually rich source of in-depth data and findings which we have, all
along, applied to assisting similarly afflicted youngsters who are
not in our direct care and to developing preventive measures.
This latter work is a part of our Extension Service and takes
many forms. In all, it involves well over 100 educators who serve
a child population of thousands, from infants and toddlers to high
schoolers who are parents themselves. But it is not the number
of participants that makes this work so helpful to them and to us,
but the ability to establish close and mutually respectful working
relationships as they stay with us for years and work with the
same child analyst. This cooperative venture is a second, different, but very important source of data and findings. It enables us
to view our relatively small sample of patients in the context of
the wider and "normal" community and to pinpoint similarities
and differences. We learn about the incidence of abuse in a variety of ethnic, racial, and socioeconomic groups, about the many
manifest symptoms in which it presents itself, and the many ways
in which it comes to the attention of parents and professionals.
It helps us to understand better how they, in turn, react to the
topic of sexual abuse and to the individual abused child who is
in their care, what implications this carries for their management
of these children, and how this contributes to the victim's experience after the abuse.

Since both our direct and indirect work with sexually abused
children has been carried on for over 40 years, the question
most commonly posed to us is "Are there more sexually abused
children now than a generation ago?" I shall begin to answer it
by relating some of our experiences.

The children referred to our Center and School suffer from
a variety of emotional difficulties, ranging from very mild to
quite severe ones. They are not referred because they suffered
sexual abuse. Even in the very rare cases where the parents know
of, or suspect, such experiences they do not view them as the
cause of their child's disturbance. Thus, the finding that there
was abuse or that there is a direct relationship between the abuse
and the manifest problems, emerges slowly through the treatment
work and through our observations of the child in the therapeutic
school setting. On my arrival in 1952, my first patient turned out
to have been sexually abused, then a very disturbed three-year-
old, now a functioning woman in her midforties (E. Furman,

1956). In all the years between, my colleagues and I have carried at least one abused patient at any one time. Through cooperative study of our experiences, we have improved our diagnostic and therapeutic understanding. In 1985, R. A. Furman reported that his inquiries showed that about 10 percent of our Center and School cases were sexually abused children, but that the ratio was considerably higher in private psychoanalytic practice.

When I began to consult in day nurseries, also in the early fifties, it was not long before sexually abused children came to my attention. I suspect there were more than I was able to diagnose. Nowadays we miss fewer such cases diagnostically and we hear about many more children by working with more professionals from different settings, many of whom have also learned to assess more accurately. And, of course, many more very young children are in daycare.

All of this may make it seem as if there are more cases, but actually there are not. As with our Center and School patients, the ratio remains constant. Also, whenever I have worked with sexually abused patients, I have learned that at least one of their parents had been abused as a child. The educators I work with, likewise, often report that many parents of their sexually abused youngsters spontaneously admit their own similar early experiences in a direct or indirect way. de Mause's (1974, 1992) studies on the sexual abuse of children worldwide show us that, sadly, this misuse is neither new nor limited to our society. Insofar as the child population that comes to our attention is concerned, the incidence of sexual abuse of children has remained essentially the same. Perhaps the more important and more difficult question is "Can we help to break the generational cycle?" One thing is new in recent years: the community's awareness of and focus on sexual abuse; so are the resulting administrative and professional regulations for reporting as well as attempts to intervene. Although the intent of these measures is good, in practice they are sometimes helpful and sometimes counterproductive, the topic we shall now begin to address.

DETECTING AND HANDLING CASES OF SEXUAL ABUSE

The following vignettes come from our work with educators and concern only the early age groups.

In my "Working with Toddlers" course two skilled care-givers were concerned about a two-year-old girl in their daycare group. She had been with them for many months and seemed to progress well in spite of some difficulties. Recently, however, she had begun to bite and wet or almost wet, dashing to the bathroom. She would "out of the blue" bite a boy, and it always was a boy, and then either flood herself with urine or run to the toilet. She had a completely bland facial expression when she did it and remained blank when the caretakers reproached her, tried to question her, or comforted the victim. She had also be-come listless, less interested in activities. She sometimes had sudden tantrums, and was unable to be comforted in her ex-hausted state afterward. Typically, the caretakers had had no idea what might be wrong to start with, but as they told of their observations, a look of shock came over their faces. They recog-nized what they had learned in discussing similar cases. "The blank look," they said, "it isn't even her. She was done to." They were able to bring it to the mother in such a way that she could contain it, listen to her child, and trace the event—a week-end with relatives where the child slept with a pre-teen boy cousin. Mother and child went on to get good professional help. The girl appeared to resume normal functioning within a few months and the teacher-parent relationship benefited, enabling them to work more closely on other concerns regarding the child.

In the course "Nursery School Children with Difficulties" an experienced head teacher in a day nursery reported the follow-ing concern about her four-year-old pupil who had entered the group several months before: His parents had separated when the boy was about two. Mother had gone to work and James was placed in home daycare with a woman who also cared for her own children. When James became old enough to be enrolled in our teacher's day nursery, the mother transferred him. She cooperated well with this nursery's expectation of a gradual sepa-ration adjustment period, and the boy settled in without signs of trouble, except that he would not eat with the group. The teacher attributed this to his missing of his mother and perhaps different rules and foods at his previous placement.

She addressed these issues with James, offered him a seat next to her, sympathized with his uncomfortable feeling, but all to no avail. She became more concerned, and this prompted her bringing it up for discussion, when she observed that the mere approach of eating time or the mention of food caused him to become bodily quite rigid with a frozen terrified look on his face. One time, when the teacher was firmer in expecting him at least to come to the table, he gagged and nearly threw up. She also observed that, although he was quite good with activities on his own, he could not take in instructions, looked away when spoken to and stiffened.

As she told her story, one of the course participants said, "Someone forced something down his mouth." The teacher affirmed that this felt right. Inquiry after that with James's mother revealed that he was very picky about his food at home, that mother in fact spent much time preparing special and different foods for him each night and even then could not always get him to eat, but he got enough taking bits of snacks on the go. Mother felt bad and was angry, attributing these fads to his wish for more time with her. She added that, for some months now, he also had not let her sleep, waking her with bad dreams or with groans and cries in his sleep from which she could not rouse him.

Mother was shocked at the teacher's intimation that something may have happened to him. It took several months before the teacher could help her to integrate the idea, but she ultimately did and got professional help when the child had an anxiety attack during a chance meeting with the prior sitter's teenaged son.

In my "Consultation Group" of co-op nursery directors, one participant reported on a girl of five in her pre-K group which met for two hours daily. The child was bright but could not concentrate on learning tasks or play in a neutral manner. She would forever focus on one goal only, to get a partner to giggle and whisper with excitedly and, in spite of the teacher's efforts at supervision, she would find a way of absenting herself with another child into a hiding place where they touched and bumped bodies and lifted or took off their clothes. She could seduce any boy, but some were easy favorite targets.

The teacher had talked about school rules of privacy, had pointed out Jennifer's missing out on learning and feeling good about achievements. She had asked the other children not to participate and to call her for help. She had also told Jennifer that perhaps she had questions about people's bodies and could

ask her mother in words instead of showing them at school by
doing. Mother and Jennifer appeared to have a somewhat overly
affectionate but not inappropriately excited relationship, and Jennifer never behaved that way when mother was in the classroom
as helper, as all co-op mothers are required to do about once a
month. It was the drivenness of Jennifer's behavior and total
disregard of all attempts to modify it that alarmed the teacher.

In discussing the case, we all felt that these characteristics
and the different behavior with Mother suggested that the child
was not just mildly overstimulated in a general way but had
been sexually played with. In talking with the mother on earlier
occasions she had either minimized the trouble or pointed the
finger at the boy peers, and she had admonished Jennifer to ''play
nicely'' at school. But she had evidently also begun to watch a
bit more closely and was alarmed to find Jennifer in their yard
with an exposed little neighbor boy. It was at this point that the
teacher voiced her suspicion to mother. Now the mother could
hear, and when she asked Jennifer who might be playing these
games with her, Jennifer revealed that grandfather played ''cozy
games.'' He lived alone in a separate part of the house, but
sometimes took care of Jennifer. With the teacher's help, the
mother discussed Grandpa's ''trouble'' with Jennifer. He stopped
babysitting and soon moved to a nursing home. Jennifer improved but never had professional help.

When I worked with a daycare program for schoolchildren
who attended before and after school hours, the staff brought up
this child for consultation: John was almost eight, but still in first
grade in the adjacent public school. His mother had come here
from another state during the previous year, separating from her
husband. She held a responsible professional job and put in long
hours, but her behavior at the center was most inappropriate as
she tried to befriend the female staff in an intimate way and paid
little heed to her son racing around and later bothering others in
the parking lot instead of getting into their car. John's impulsive
restlessness and lack of academic interests made him a problem
pupil to his first-grade teacher.

In the daycare setting he could be more or less contained
by the director who literally had him in tow all the time, even
keeping him in her office when she needed to work there for brief
periods. The moment he felt himself to be not fully attended, he

broke loose, teased his peers by invading their space or grabbing things from them. But most specifically, and always suddenly, he would run up behind a boy and jump on him, bending him down with his stranglehold till staff forcibly pulled him off his victim.

The mother responded to the director's concern with "Boys will be boys," but she added that her husband used to roughhouse a lot with John when he cared for him during her working hours. She said that she had left her husband because of his drug habits and "perverse" behavior. Following a brief holiday vacation, John's behavior became much worse and there were a few incidents of smearing in the bathroom. It turned out the father had stayed with the family. The mother agreed that this was not a good influence, but she could not protect John nor could she intervene in John's newly struck up "friendship" with a couple of teenagers. The boys' vandalism had brought complaints from neighbors.

After further class discussion the director told the mother that she would need to report her for neglect unless the child's home care improved. It did improve, but within a short time the mother withdrew John and moved away. We felt the boy had been abused, his humping behavior and smearing of stools point to bodily invasive experiences.

Well known and evident also in some of the above examples is the abused child's driven need to do to others actively what he or she had suffered passively. The involvement of specific bodily zones (mouth, anus, or genitals) has also proven to be an important diagnostic clue. There are, however, other by now well-known syndromes, for example, tics and bizarre movements which are often misdiagnosed and treated as neurological illness or "chemical imbalance in the nervous system." Several such cases have been reported by teachers, and we have seen this among our patients as a response to sexual abuse.

Even as we have learned to be on the alert to a variety of manifest behaviors, we know from our patients that the disturbance resulting from sexual abuse may affect functioning in much subtler ways, especially when the abuse occurred during the earliest years, producing atypical and post-traumatic pathology (E. Furman, 1985, 1986b, 1988). We also find quite often that patients referred to us as "hyperactive" or "attention deficit disorder'' are actually suffering from the effects of sexual abuse. In these masked forms, however, the differential diagnosis cannot be made from the teachers' observations, but requires individual therapeutic work.

We have learned further from our patients and observations in our School that some quite specific diagnostic behaviors, namely, perverse actions such as tying oneself up, never show at school and are rarely reported to the teacher. By contrast, overwhelming experiences that occurred away from home and in the absence of the parents may not manifest themselves at home, but can be triggered into action when the child enters a group setting where he feels relatively safe (Benkendorf, 1969; E. Furman, 1978b).

THE EDUCATOR'S TASK

The above vignettes illustrate that the educators' first task is to observe their charges in such a way that they can recognize the experience, or likely experience, of sexual abuse and to tolerate this knowledge in a containing way. Only then can they use it to empathize with the child, to handle his or her behavior thoughtfully, and to bring it to the parents in a calm, containing way so that the parents in turn will be able to assist the child. This usually includes guiding them to seek and carry through with therapeutic help as well as reporting in some instances.

Making an effective referral, i.e., not only suggesting a competent professional, but assisting parents to involve themselves and the child in therapy, is at best a difficult task. If it involves reporting, the task is not made easier, but need not be jeopardized. Both therapists and educators have found it helpful to report with the knowledge and cooperation of the parents or to assist them with self-reporting. If this process fails at any point along the way, the child may not be helped or may even incur additional suffering. Such failure may be caused by the educator and/or parent needing to deny the reality of abuse, responding to their shock with excitement or punitiveness toward the child, or with anger at each other, or with interruption of contact due to the child being withdrawn from the center.

The key to helpful intervention rests not merely with contained knowledge, but with whether the teacher has been able to establish cooperative and mutually respectful relationships with the children's parents. Such relationships are the crucial context in which difficult topics can be addressed and worked on. This is an area where the psychoanalytic teacher or consultant proves most helpful. When he or she has been able to establish such a trusting working relationship with the educators, they, in turn, find it easier to build similar relationships with the parents. It also helps them to identify with the analyst's contained, empathic, and realistic approach so that they can tolerate their own insight, integrate it with the knowledge the analyst contributes, and use it in talking with the parent. When a teacher reports back on her conference with the parent, I often hear echoes of the way the topic was approached in our Course or Consultation Group. For example, "Jennifer has seemed so overwhelmed lately. She tries so hard to do the right thing, but it feels like something gets in her way. Have you noticed this at home, or any other changes? What do you think of it? How can we make sense of it and help her?" Insofar as the relationship, or chain of relationships, works, a considerable number of cases are helped, but, of course, there are also failures. A failure, however, cannot be judged as such right away. Sometimes parents return to the teacher for help at a later time and sometimes teachers meet a parent by chance years later and learn that help was sought out and used when the child got older. The initial discussion can then be seen to have laid a helpful groundwork.

PREVENTIVE MEASURES

The Pitfalls of Active Teaching

The community's heightened awareness of incidents of sexual abuse of children also heightened concern. Parents', educators', and mental health professionals' urgent desire to prevent such occurrences, and to protect especially the youngest children who are most easily victimized, prompted many to opt for an immediate, very active approach. Its basic aim was to *inform* youngsters, to teach them what constitutes sexual abuse ("good" touching and ''bad'' touching), to instruct them how potential abusers talk and act, and to urge them to keep away from such people or to rebuff their approaches. Not only parents and teachers have tried to impress children with these lessons, but so have counselors, police, and newly trained specialists, as well as numerous TV programs, tapes, and books, often with graphic illustrations.

The results of these efforts have all too often proved counterproductive. Parents, teachers, and caregivers reported numerous incidents of children becoming scared of the wrong things, for example, of going to sleep, of the dark, of going upstairs, or of speaking to anyone. More alarmingly, some children coped with their upset by turning it into excitement and a need to do before they might be done to, as shown in the following experience.

One day I received a distressed phone call from a day nursery director, one of our Course participants. During the preceding few days she had been contacted by several parents whose children had run off on excited forays in the neighborhood to track down imaginary molesters, and some were newly engaged in mutual sexual play. Discussion in our seminar revealed that the other participants' centers had encountered similar troubles. It all started the day after a TV program on teaching children about sexual abuse and what they should do to avoid it. Although viewing with parents had been suggested, many parents were not home or looked in only sporadically on the child's viewing. The youngsters' behavioral response was prompted by their unmastered anxiety. The educators proceeded to help them and their parents in those terms.

Such unhappy experiences serve as a reminder that not only for some, but for all children, sexual abuse is an idea fraught with intense feelings (feelings that are not dispelled, but often heightened by intellectual knowledge and moral prohibitions) and that to protect oneself from a great danger is a very big responsibility, one that young children are afraid of and indeed cannot shoulder on their own.

The Role of Supervision

Parents know that their child's self-care, self-protection, and self-control depend for many years on parental presence and emotional availability and on their direct supervision, even when the child knows what is expected and has learned what to do. Preschoolers have usually been told and know to be cautious of road traffic, but this does not mean that they can be trusted to keep safe on their own. All young children, preschool and even during the early elementary school years, need consistent supervision by their parents or parent substitutes, not only in strange surroundings, but in their familiar neighborhoods where most incidents of sexual abuse happen.

Doing What the Parents Do

Taking over the care and protection of our bodies and achieving mastery of impulses and feelings is a slow, gradual process that takes place in the context of the relationship with loved ones, and hinges more on what they do in ongoing everyday interactions than on what they say in specific lessons. This is as true with other areas of self-care, such as eating, dressing, toileting, coping with hurts, and learning to avoid common dangers, as it is with protecting oneself from undue sexual stimulation, intrusion, and attack. We have learned that the children who do eventually become independently safe in regard to traffic, for example, are not the ones who were allowed to go out on their own and who received lectures and warnings about the dangers of cars, but those who in the company of the parents, day in and out, observed and gradually identified with their attitudes about, and behavior, in the street—where and how they crossed, what they looked for, how they gauged the distance of oncoming cars.

Equally important are the parents' attitudes and actions in regard to teaching protection from potential sexual abuse. This shows very prominently in the ways they delegate responsibility for their child to substitutes. How do they select, get to know, and check on a babysitter? Before parents allow their child to visit a peer's home, do they visit that home with their child or ask the other parents and child to come over for a visit, so that they can get a clearer idea of that family's home rules and trustworthiness? Do parents let their children play outside, unsupervised, by themselves or with other children, or do they insist on adequate adult supervision at all times? The child will note whether or not, and how carefully, the parents evaluate each situation and each potential parent substitute, or whether they go by superficial impressions and hearsay. Most abusers are superficially "nice" and most of them are not total strangers, but persons to whom the parents unwittingly delegate the child's care, or who have access to the child when no adult is supervising closely enough.

Children similarly observe how their parents interact with strangers in the street and stores, whom they avoid, with whom they talk, and how intimate such contacts become. Just how astutely children observe and draw their conclusions from all this is exemplified by Annie noting an inconsistency in her otherwise most appropriately careful mother. When her father hosted a Christmas reception in the home, Annie was initially introduced. Soon mother found her sitting in the men's laps and cuddling up to them. Taken aback and concerned by this unusual intimacy, the mother took Annie aside and reprimanded her, but Annie replied that Mom herself had just recently encouraged her to sit on the lap of an altogether strange man and even to kiss him, so she figured it was O.K. with Dad's friends. And what was Annie referring to? A visit with a Santa Claus at the department store! This mother recognized the confusion she had created and clarified her mistake to Annie. How often do we fail to respect and support our children's healthy beginning reticence and, instead, encourage them to embrace someone they do not know, to please us, perhaps to fulfill an old wish from our own childhood, or to impress someone with their friendliness?

Self-protection through Self-care

This brings us to the other aspect of learning self-protection, that of guarding our body against undue intimacy. When a mother lovingly cares for her baby's body, she not only feeds and cleans him, but her intimate handling makes him feel good, makes him like her and what she does with him, and helps him get to like his body and know it as his own. Pretty soon the infant gets to enjoy other ways of being close with mother (singing and babbling, playing little games, following her around). Instead of being cared for, he increasingly wants to do for himself (feed, wash, wipe, and dress himself) and often becomes quite adamant in resisting her bodily ministrations. Although this drive for "me all by myself" is often a bother, a mother generally welcomes her child's need for autonomy and patiently helps him toward self-care (E. Furman, 1992, 1993). In the process, he takes over her attitude of respectful nonintrusiveness and privacy in regard to intimate bodily matters.

At the start of nursery school, children usually have mastered basic self-care, use mother only for the more difficult tasks, and are reluctant to let outsiders, even teachers, take this role. For example, if their mothers are not there to tie the hood or shoes, many children would prefer to leave them undone. When an older girl approached three-year-old Kevin on the playground offering to push him on the swing, his mother was somewhat surprised, but glad, to hear him say, "No, only my Mommy and I do things for me." She realized that this healthy sense of "hands off me" would help him to protect himself from interference or intrusions by others. However, this valuable sense of inviolable body ownership does not develop readily when the mother fails to respond to the child's wish to do for himself, or when she handles his body intrusively, or when she ministers to his bodily needs in front of others, ignoring his right to privacy, such as undressing him and changing his diapers where others can see him.

The Role of the Relationship

The development of bodily self-protection is also endangered when several people minister to the infant's and toddler's bodily care, especially when these people are not even known to the mother, or she has not personally transferred her child to them, as unfortunately happens in many child care centers, where a succession of assistants may take over from the primary mother substitute during changing shifts on long days. Also, especially in programs with inadequate staff-child ratios, young children may be lonely away from their mothers and long for loving closeness. The following vignette illustrates the dangers inherent in loneliness and longing.

During a seminar of my "Working with Toddlers" course the discussion focused on toileting of toddlers in daycare centers.

A new but observant and thoughtful member of our group described how happily many toddlers line up to be diapered by her on the changing table which stands along one wall of their room. Some wet repeatedly, just to be changed it seemed, some lined up even when they were dry, and with some the assistant caregiver goes around to feel their bottoms for wetness and then brings them over for cleanup. The caregiver reflected that the children like to be diapered because it affords the most intimate one-to-one relationship during their day at the center. She added how sad it was that such should be the case. We addressed the children's stimulation by exposure to observing the sexual differences, by the repeated bottom-touching, and by their passive lying-down position as opposed to changing diapers while the child stands and can participate actively. I was struck mainly by the difference between these lonely children who offer up their privates for love and the toddlers who attend with their mothers in our Toddler Group and reserve all bodily care so strictly for mother that they even reject a familiar and liked teacher's offer of tying the strings of their painting apron. Some toddlers, of course, simply resist being changed. That can be a nuisance to the adult, but it shows a healthy sense of body ownership and self-protection against intrusion.

Thus, through our ways of caring for the child's body, we may either help him develop self-protection against abuse or we may unwittingly foster the opposite.

CONCLUSION

If we protect our children and help them develop self-protection while they are little, they will not need our verbal lessons and warnings. If we leave young children unsupervised or delegate with less than utmost care, or if our handling conveys indifference to their bodily privacy and interferes with their developing sense of ownership, no amount of lecturing will counteract it. We need to give thought to these indirect, but much more effective, measures of helping children prevent sexual abuse.

14

Referring a Child for Special Help

LUANE RAIA LASKY
and
EDWARD J. SCHIFF, M.D.

Editor's note: Since the late sixties, the Cleveland Center for Research in Child Development has offered the preschool educators in our community a service called "Consultation Groups." Such a group consists of four directors/head teachers who meet with one of our child psychoanalysts every other week for one and a half hours. Their self-chosen topics encompass a wide range, including discussion of individual children with difficulties, to gain understanding and help with management, educational policies, work with parents, administrative issues, and aspects of child development in general. To assure an optimum of shared interests and experience, each group's participants are in charge of similar facilities, such as co-ops, private nursery schools, daycare centers. Most consultation groups meet regularly for many years and provide much appreciated opportunities for joint learning, which contributes to professional growth, improved preschool settings, and help to the children and their families. Sometimes a group decides to share what they have learned by writing an article.

The topic of referral of children with difficulties crops up in most consultation groups when discussion has pinpointed a child's need for help beyond the school's scope. The accounts in the following sections resulted from the concomitant but sepa-rate work of two consultation groups. The first was a group of director/teachers of cooperative preschools, and its report was prepared by one of the participants, Luane Raia Lasky. The sec-ond was a group of directors of private preschools, and its report was written by their consultant, Edward J. Schiff, M.D.

A Teacher's Role in Guiding Parents Toward a Referral

LUANE RAIA LASKY

Referring a child for professional help is always a painful process. To a child who already has difficulties in dealing with his environment, referral means encountering new people in places strange to him, and it means undergoing unfamiliar procedures to which he must adjust in his already precariously balanced world. For the teacher there is anxiety for the child and his feelings, the stress of working with the child and his parents, as well as additional concern for the other children in the classroom.

But it is the parent to whom referral is probably the most painful. Suggestions of referring their child can only heighten the concern which may already be present, and augment the feeling that somehow they have failed as parents. They may feel threatened and the teacher's suggestions may be interpreted as criticism. Referral brings a host of practical problems to parents which must seem overwhelming—the selection of the proper person or agency for the initial evaluation, the possible financial drain, time and transportation difficulties, and the effect of these changes on other family members may all be sources of further anxiety. A wise teacher tries to be as cognizant of the parents' stress in this difficult time as, it is hoped, the parents will be of their child's hardship.

The teacher's task in guiding parents toward referral is simplified immeasurably if the parents are already aware of their child's difficulties, present their concerns to the teacher, and realize the urgency of the need for professional help. Then her job is to suggest the agency or individual she feels would provide the type of evaluation most relevant to the child's particular difficulties. It helps, of course, if the teacher is able to recommend a specific person to the parents, a professional whose work is known to the teacher. This can help smooth the way for the parents. Good communication among parent, teacher, and the person doing the evaluation can help parents cope with any misunderstandings that may come at this time.

A less ideal but a workable situation arises when the child's difficulties, as presented by the teacher, are readily recognized and acknowledged by concerned parents. The teacher may then act as the catalyst in bringing the parents to the realization of their child's need for more help than they or the school can give. The case of four-and-a-half-year-old Andrew may help to illustrate this type of situation.

THE CASE OF ANDREW

From the very first day of school Andrew's teacher observed that he was different from the other children, although his mother had not indicated this in her initial interview. Andrew could handle his bodily needs well, but always was an outsider in the children's activities, involved in doing his "own thing." While others would sit and wait to be served, Andrew would grab his cracker, drink his juice, and demand more before other children were served. Block-building was disastrous for him, since he would play next to but not *with* the others, and grab blocks for his own use from the other children's work. Consequently, the others would avoid playing with him. He would often become highly absorbed in a table activity, pursue it on his own, and then suddenly jump up and run around the room and into the hallway, startling the children close to him. Similar behavior would manifest itself during story time or show-and-tell, when Andrew would again jump up, run around the room, grab the rhythm instruments or bang on the piano, always demanding the attention of the teacher. He was not able to share with the children, and if he did not have his way, he would snatch the desired object away from the others.

Andrew had an excellent vocabulary, a good memory, and on his own enjoyed writing the entire alphabet in upper case on the blackboard. His speech, however, was sing-song, and he pronounced words laboriously, syllable by syllable, as if he were reading them. He was not able to handle scissors or paste well, or even to paint adequately at the easel. His small muscle activity appeared to be at a minimal level of development for his age. In order to work more effectively with the other children, his teacher would often ask the working mother to remove Andrew from the group to another area, and work with him on a one-to-one basis so that he would not disturb the rest of the class.

When the teacher first talked with Andrew's mother about his behavior, she was told, "My doctor said I shouldn't say anything—the teachers would find out soon enough." The mother then related some of the stresses at home prior to Andrew's admission: his baby sister had worn a cast on her arm for an extended period of time, his father had undergone surgery, and a close relative had died within the preceding year. Andrew's mother recognized his problems—his nearly constant activity, clumsiness on the large muscle equipment, and lack of small muscle coordination. She admitted that she was unable to cope with him at times and that she would lose patience with him.

Since the teacher of the school had participated in a consultation group, she presented Andrew's problems for discussion to the group, with the parents' permission. A recommendation was made to refer Andrew for an evaluation. The director then had a conference with Andrew's mother to discuss his present status in the classroom, and to suggest possible ways of handling him in school and at home.

There appeared to be a slight conflict between mother and father over handling Andrew at home, but both had enough interest in and concern about their child to list Andrew's positive and negative points of behavior, which they shared with the teacher. Andrew's mother stated midway through the conference that she felt that, as parents, they needed help—she was at her "wit's end" in handling him. Fortunately, the teacher was able to build on this and to suggest that the parents contact Dr. P. for an appointment for an evaluation and recommendation. Dr. P. was a staff member at a local agency who had a fine record of working competently and sensitively with parents, children, and preschools. Within a week's time the initial appointment was made, and Andrew's parents began their series of interviews. Dr. P. contacted the school for information on Andrew's behavior in the classroom. Andrew underwent psychological testing. This all took time. At the end of three months it was recommended that the parents contact a therapeutic school for help. Andrew's mother, however, was not able to accept this recommendation. She discussed it with the teacher, who encouraged her to explore the possibility of continued work with the suggested agency. When the parents were still unable to accept the specific recommendation after additional conferences with the teacher, they were supported in seeking help from another but comparable source, and followed through with it. The parents' good relationship with the teacher helped them to accept their child's need for a referral and to weather the upsets of a psychiatric evaluation and recommended treatment.

How much more difficult the teacher's task becomes if, unlike Andrew's mother and father, the parents seem oblivious to any problem, and appear to be taken totally by surprise upon learning of the teacher's concern for their child's inability to function within "normal" limits in the school environment! Perhaps these parents have had no chance to observe him in a setting where his difficulties would be obvious, or they may have noticed his problems but may have denied the reality of his troubles, as John's parents did.

THE CASE OF JOHN

Outwardly John was a very happy, carefree four-year-old who approached everyone in a very friendly manner and had no apparent qualms about mother's leaving after the first few days of school. The teacher remembered that on his initial visit to the classroom in the preceding spring, John was very quiet and appeared too shy to speak. Consequently his mother did much of the talking for him with the other children. Now that the mother was gone, however, the teacher noticed that when John tried to communicate with the children, many correct sounds were nonexistent, and his voice was guttural in tone. He seemed to rely primarily on facial expressions or hand movements to get his message across.

John's coordination was awkward. He stumbled a lot and tripped over things easily, his balance was poor, and his small motor control was minimal. He had difficulty concentrating for any length of time, and at times would have a blank look in his eyes, despite a fixed grin on his face. His play centered around the kitchen area, especially the sink—in fact, wherever there was water, there John could be found (even at the fishbowl on the science table). In other areas John also lagged developmentally and the teacher suspected, after further observation, that John was mentally retarded.

She tried to recall her first parent-teacher conference with the mother, checked through the child's medical form and personal history data sheet—nowhere could she find any indication from the parents or the doctor that retardation was a possibility. How to approach the parents without shocking them or arousing antagonism became her basic concern.

The teacher decided to begin with something that was quite apparent to all: John's lack of speech development—even though his mother had definitely minimized this problem at the first conference by stating only, "John's speech is a little slow. . . ."

During the first month of school, John's mother brought him and took him home. The teacher made a point of developing a friendly rapport with the mother in these few moments each day. Occasionally she would say something such as, "You did such a good job preparing John for nursery school," or "John seems very happy at school. You have been very supportive to him in these first weeks." When the teacher felt the time was ripe, she approached the mother asking for a brief conference. "John has difficulty communicating with the other children. I looked at his medical form, and there is no indication of physical difficulty in this area. I'm wondering if you could give me some more information. Could we set up a few moments some time to talk about this?" The mother agreed.

Mrs. H. was very nervous and apprehensive at this meeting when she first entered, but gradually relaxed and was able to acknowledge that she, too, had noticed the difference between John's speech and that of the other children. She then mentioned spontaneously that she had never given it much thought before because she always understood what he meant, and since he had not walked until nearly two years of age, she had just assumed that he was a little "slow" in developing. She added that John's birth had been difficult, but did not go into more detail. When asked if the doctor had ever noticed or commented about John's speech and "slowness," the mother replied, "No." The teacher mentioned that she was concerned about John's speech and she did not feel equipped to evaluate the problem adequately. At this point the mother said musingly, "Perhaps we should have him tested," and then hastily added, "Maybe the city's speech therapist could do this for us. . . . " It was impossible to tell at this point if the mother, in the recesses of her mind, was questioning John's mental abilities, and perhaps was beginning to consider the possibility of retardation. At any rate, the teacher felt that the suggestion for a full evaluation might be too threatening to the mother at this time. She therefore agreed that a speech evaluation would be a good idea. The mother decided to make the necessary arrangements. The teacher felt the willingness of John's mother to take the initiative in setting up this interview was an encouraging development.

The recommendation of the speech therapist was that there was a developmental lag in speech and language, but that there appeared to be difficulties in other areas of growth also, and a more comprehensive evaluation might provide some answers for the worried parents. The parents' concern was very obvious to the teacher now. She was able to help them understand that while there was a definite problem, there was something they could do to help John. She asked if they would be willing to have John tested at a particular local agency, a place where competent psychologists, doctors, and social workers could evaluate John's overall development. The parents agreed after inquiring about the procedures of initial visits and costs. The teacher then gave the parents the name, address, and telephone number of this agency and tried to be as encouraging as possible. By the time the conversation was over, the parents seemed to be in a more positive frame of mind. The teacher did not know just when the mother would call the agency (or even if she would have second thoughts about it); however, she called the agency herself and relayed what had transpired to one of the social workers, in preparation for the mother's call, asking that she be given all possible assistance. The mother did call the agency within a week, and testing was begun, as well as counseling with the parents.

THE PARENT-TEACHER RELATIONSHIP

John's case shows clearly that it takes time to build a teacher-parent relationship with enough confidence in the teacher for the parents to accept the idea of a referral without feeling threatened or criticized. Suggesting a referral prematurely could be a real detriment to establishing rapport with the parents, as well as to effecting a successful referral. To "make haste slowly" can be a delicate task! Gathering information, developing a relationship with the parents, and working with the child and parents all take thoughtful preparation on the part of the teacher.

The task is not completed when the suggestion for referral is made, but rather when the parents have been aided in following through and in embarking on the recommended course of treatment. During these trying weeks and months most parents need their child's teacher as a professional friend they can turn to, and rely on, to talk things over and to gain encouragement.

There will be times when an attempt to effect a referral will be unsuccessful. This can be very frustrating to the teacher. But even when the attempt to guide toward an evaluation has been thwarted by the parents' unwillingness or inability to acknowledge the need for help, a seed may have been planted that may enable the parents to accept the idea of referral at a later date.

What Failures in Referral
Have Taught Us

EDWARD J. SCHIFF, M.D.

Referring a child from a community nursery school to an appropriate professional person or facility for evaluation and/or treatment of his difficulties can be a most rewarding task for all
concerned, or it can be a most frustrating, painful, time-consum-
ing, unhappy effort which may well end in failure. Between these
two extremes there is often a mixture of reward and frustration,
of pleasure for the child who may now be receiving some needed
help, or of despair when the help is unavailable or insufficient, or
when we cannot even help the parents to take the necessary steps.

During the 10 years of our consultation group's regular
meetings we frequently found ourselves struggling, sometimes
for months, with the very knotty problems associated with referrals. Our struggles were successful at least insofar as we learned
a lot from one another, and some of our most unhappy referral
failures taught us a great deal. Through them we gained understanding of some general principles which we could put to use
when similar situations were again brought to our attention. The
following brief vignettes, graciously supplied by members of our
consultation group, illustrate some of the knowledge we have
gained.

CLINICAL EXAMPLES

A three-and-a-half-year-old girl who was first placed in a five-
day four- to-five-year old group, was shifted to a younger, three-
day a week group after a week's observation and extensive discussion with the mother who was very upset and felt that her
child had failed. The little girl spoke very little, stood in front

of her cubby without removing her coat, and appeared terrified. She had attended a different preschool earlier where similar problems had been noted. While she made some progress in certain school activities during the year, she never spoke spontaneously. If the mother said, "Now say thus or so," she would do so. Much effort was devoted to helping the mother deal with her great upset and guilt over a number of observations, and many attempts were made to engage her. Despite her seemingly genuine concern, however, the mother never really allowed herself to become involved in helping her daughter cope with troubles, not even with her prominent separation difficulty. Although she finally did talk to a professional person on one occasion, she was never able to follow through, nor could she discuss this consultation with the school. After one year she withdrew her child and entered her in another school, only to repeat the cycle. This failure in being able to help such an appealing little girl was very difficult for the staff.

Another example of failure in effecting a referral concerned a little girl, four years old, whose mother had been recently divorced in another city where the father still remained. Mother and child were living with her parents in our area. The child's confusion was greatly exacerbated by frequent travels to visit her father in the sole company of her paternal grandparents whom she hardly knew. This resulted in a severe separation problem, with the child terrified at being left by the mother in any circumstance. Many efforts were made to refer this mother and child for help in dealing with the divorce, the separation, and the mother's working, all to no avail.

Finally, here is an example of what had seemed a failure but worked out well in the end. This four-year-old girl entered preschool with a series of difficult behavioral and physical problems which frequently proved quite disruptive to the class. There were many discussions with the parents by both teacher and director, and repeated discussions in the consultation group. Finally, the teacher and director were able to build a sufficiently strong and positive relationship with both parents so that after two years, and some months prior to entering kindergarten, the parents could accept a referral. It proved to be most successful and helpful to the child. Here, time and patience, skill and tact, finally won the day.

PRINCIPLES IN EFFECTING REFERRALS

What we learned, or were constantly relearning, were some basic principles found to be most helpful in initiating referrals.

It is usually advisable to begin the process with the mother, or mothering person, because of her intimate closeness with and knowledge of her young child. In time, both parents need to be involved to assist them in thinking things through together and supporting one another. Individual situations vary, however, and our choice of approach must take that into consideration.

The concept of referral is easily understood by the psychologically sophisticated parent, and little explanation of what a referral entails is needed. At the other end of the scale, explaining the concept of referral to a psychologically quite unsophisticated parent can be an arduous task indeed. We found, however, that psychological sophistication was no guarantee that the referral would be easily accomplished, nor was psychological naïvete an assurance of failure. Strong emotional resistances against recognizing a need for help are shared by all parents, from the most sophisticated to the psychologically least knowledgeable. The threat to the parents', especially the mother's, self-esteem and their often painful guilt in needing to acknowledge that their child has a problem frequently underlies these resistances.

We found that our most valuable tools for assuring successful referrals were: (1) the *relationship* the teacher and/or director were able to establish with the parent(s), and (2) the willingness of the staff to be patient and take as much *time* as was needed. This could be anywhere from a few weeks to as much as two years. Some parents were only willing to accept a referral when their denial of the problem was at least dented by the imminence of entry to the public school kindergarten.

Effecting a referral is a process in which the preschool professional engages the parent(s) by using a variety of available means. These may include: sharing significant observations with the parents; involving mother and/or father by having them observe in the classroom; conferences with the teacher and/or director, and conferences in which the teacher and director meet with the parents; discussing with the parents the intention of bringing the problem to the consultation group for preliminary assessment and suggestions, and asking for their permission to do so. Sometimes relevant books may be used to engage the parents' interest and cooperation. Books, however, are never more than an adjunct and, in cases of strong resistance, may be useless or worse.

All these means, and it is hoped many others, take a great deal of time, compassion, and tact, and are a part of the ongoing task of building a relationship with the parents which, in turn, might facilitate the referral.

There is a last, but by no means least, very helpful factor in making successful referrals. It is the director's working relationship with several child development specialists in the community. Parents are much more willing to contact a specific person their director knows and can recommend because she has had many positive experiences in referring other parents. Moreover, a specialist who knows and respects the director is more likely to take into account the school's observations and to provide suggestions for helping the child in the preschool setting.

References

Bain, A. J. K., & Barnett, L. E. (1980), *The Design of a Day Care System in a Nursery Setting for Children Under Five*. London: Tavistock Institute of Human Relations.

Benkendorf, J. (1969), Case 3: Martin. In: *The Therapeutic Nursery School*, ed. R. A. Furman & A. Katan. New York: International Universities Press, pp. 156–180.

Britannica Dictionary of the English Language (1964), Chicago, IL: Encyclopeadia Britannica.

Eastman, P. D. (1960), *Are You My Mother?* New York: Random House (Beginner Books).

Egbert, E. D., Battit, G. E., Turndorf, H., & Beecher, H. K. (1963), The value of the preoperative visit by an anesthetist. *J. Amer. Med. Assn.*, 185:553–555.

———— ———— Welch, C. E., & Bartlett, M. K. (1964), Reduction of postoperative pain by encouragement and instruction of the patient—a study of doctor-patient rapport. *New Eng. J. Med.*, 270:825–827.

Freud, A. (1963), The concept of developmental lines. *The Psychoanalytic Study of the Child*, 18:245–265. New York: International Universities Press.

———— Burlingham, D. (1943), *War and Children*. New York: International Universities Press.

———— (1944), *Infants Without Families*. In: The Writings of Anna Freud, 3:541–664. New York: International Universities Press, 1973.

Freud, S. (1920), Beyond the pleasure principle. *Standard Edition*, 18:1–64. London: Hogarth Press, 1955.

Friedlander, K. (1946), Psychoanalytic orientation in child guidance work. *The Psychoanalytic Study of the Child*, 2:343–357. New York: International Universities Press.

Furman, E. (1956), An ego disturbance in a young child. *The Psychoanalytic Study of the Child*, 11:321–335. New York: International Universities Press.

———— (1967), The latency child as an active participant in the analytic work. In: *The Child Analyst at Work*, ed. E. Geleerd. New York: International Universities Press, pp. 142–184.

———— (1969a), Some thoughts on the pleasure in working. *Bull. Phila. Assn. Psychoanal.*, 19:197–212.

———— (1969b), Treatment via the mother. In: *The Therapeutic Nursery School*, ed. R. A. Furman & A. Katan. New York: International Universities Press, pp. 64–116.

———— (1974), *A Child's Parent Dies*. New Haven, CT: Yale University Press.

———— (1978a), Helping children cope with death. In: *What Nursery School Teachers Ask Us About*, ed. E. Furman. Madison, CT: International Universities Press, 1986, pp. 183–196. Aso in: *Young Children*, 33:25–32.

———— (1978b), Use of the nursery school for evaluation. In: *Child Analysis and Therapy*, ed. J. Glenn. New York: Aronson, pp. 128–159.

———— (1982), Mothers have to be there to be left. *The Psychoanalytic Study of the Child*, 37:15–28. New Haven, CT: Yale University Press.

———— (1985), On fusion, integration, and feeling good. *The Psychoanalytic Study of the Child*, 40:81–110. New Haven, CT: Yale University Press.

———— (1986a), Learning to feel good about sexual differences. In: *What Nursery School Teachers Ask Us About*, ed. E. Furman. Madison, CT: International Universities Press, pp. 101–122.

———— (1986b), On trauma: When is the death of a parent traumatic? *The Psychoanalytic Study of the Child*, 41:191–208. New Haven, CT: Yale University Press.

———— (1986c), *What Nursery School Teachers Ask Us About*. Madison, CT: International Universities Press.

———— (1987a), *Helping Young Children Grow*. Madison, CT: International Universities Press.

———— (1987b), *The Teacher's Guide to Helping Young Children Grow*. Madison, CT: International Universities Press.

———— (1988), Experiences in working with atypical children (L'expérience du travail avec des enfants atypiques). *J. Psychoanal. de l'Enfant*, 5:14–32.

———— (1991), Children of divorce. *Child Anal.*, 2:43–60.

———— (1992), *Toddlers and Their Mothers*. Madison, CT: International Universities Press.

———— (1993), *Toddlers and Their Mothers: Abridged Version for Parents and Educators*. Madison, CT: International Universities Press.

———— Furman, R. A. (1989), Some effects of the one-parent family on personality development. In: *The Problem of Loss and Mourning: Psychoanalytic Perspectives*, ed. D. R. Dietrich & P. C. Shabad. Madison, CT: International Universities Press, pp. 129–157.

Furman, R. A. (1975), *Some Thoughts About the Adult Patient's Preschool Children*. Address to the Ohio State Psychiatric Association, Cleveland, Ohio.

———— (1978), Some developmental aspects of the verbalization of affects. *The Psychoanalytic Study of the Child*, 33:187–211. New Haven, CT: Yale University Press.

———— (1985), Sexual seduction in childhood: Some child-analytic perspectives. *Child Anal.*, 5:68–78, 1994. See also Panel (1988).

———— (1986), The father-child relationship. In: *What Nursery School Teachers Ask Us About*, ed. E. Furman. Madison, CT: International Universities Press, pp. 21–34.

———— Katan, A. (1969), *The Therapeutic Nursery School*. New York: International Universities Press.

Galenson, E., & Roiphe, H. (1980), The preoedipal development of the boy. *J. Amer. Psychoanal. Assn.*, 28:805–827.

Goldsborough, J., Illustrator (1981), *I Can Do It by Myself*. New York: Golden Press.

Herzog, J. (1980), Sleep disturbance and father hunger in 18-to-28-month-old boys: The Erlkoenig syndrome. *The Psychoanalytic Study of the Child*, 35:219–236. New Haven, CT: Yale University Press.

Klaus, M. D., & Kennell, J. H. (1976), *Maternal-Infant Bonding*. St. Louis, MO: C. V. Mosby.

Krauss, R. (1945), *The Carrot Seed*. New York: Harper.

Lauter, E. (1978), Why worry helps. *Parents Magazine*, 53:40–42.

Mause, L. de (1974), The evolution of childhood. In: *The History of Childhood*, ed. L. de Mause. London: Souvenir Press, 1980, pp. 1–73.

——— (1992), The history of child assault. *Empathic Parenting*, 15:1/2:24–42.

McDonald, M. (1963), Helping children to understand death: An experience with death in a nursery school. *J. Nursery Ed.*, 19:19–25.

Panel (1988), The seduction hypothesis. A. E. Marans, reporter. *J. Amer. Psychoanal. Assn.*, 36:759–771.

Provence, S., Naylor, A., & Patterson, J. (1977), *The Challenge of Daycare*. New Haven, CT: Yale University Press.

Shengold, L. (1985), Defensive anality and anal narcissism. *Internat. J. Psycho-Anal.*, 66:47–73.

Skaar, G. (cca 1950), *The Very Little Dog*. USA: William R. Scott (Young Scott Book).

Smith, E. (1957), *The Complete Book of Absolutely Perfect Baby and Child Care*. New York : Harcourt, Brace.

Spock, B. (1946), *Common Sense Book of Baby and Child Care*. New York: Duell, Sloane & Pearce.

Tate, T. W., & Ammerman, D. L., Eds. (1979), *The Chesapeake in the Seventeenth Century—Essays on Anglo-American Society and Politics*. Chapel Hill, NC: University of North Carolina Press.

Thomas, R. D. (1977), *The Man Who Would Be Perfect*. Philadelphia, PA: University of Pennsylvania Press.

White, B. D. (1978), *The First Three Years of Life*. New York: Avon Books.

Winnicott, D. W. (1953), Transitional objects and transitional phenomena. In: *Playing and Reality*. New York: Basic Books, 1971, pp. 1–125.

——— (1958), The capacity to be alone. In: *The Maturational Processes and the Facilitating Environment*. New York: International Universities Press, 1965, pp. 29–36.

——— (1965), *The Maturational Processes and the Facilitating Environment*. New York: International Universities Press.

Name Index

Subject Index

199